ROB KING is the founder and CEO of ˮ
marketing company that specialises in hel
agencies grow their sales and revenue. ˮ
of experience in the creative industry, Rˤ
marketing and has a deep understandin
and opportunities that creatives face when it comes to growing their
business.

Rob has a proven track record of helping creative businesses
and agencies increase their sales and revenue, and has worked with
a wide range of clients in the advertising, design, film, music, and
publishing sectors. Rob is also an investor in several agencies and
creative businesses.

He has worked with some of the most well-known and respected
names in the industry, such as Abbey Road Studios, film production
companies and numerous creative agencies. In addition to this, Rob
has travelled with several UK Prime Ministers and governments on
international trade missions. He is a sought-after speaker and has
presented on sales and marketing strategies for the creative industry at
conferences and events around the world.

www.theclientkey.com

Selling Creativity

Rob King

How creatives and agencies can grow
their business through the art of Sales

SilverWood

Published in 2023 by SilverWood Books

SilverWood Books Ltd
14 Small Street, Bristol, BS1 1DE, United Kingdom
www.silverwoodbooks.co.uk

ISBN 978-1-80042-241-4 (paperback)

British Library Cataloguing in Publication Data
A CIP catalogue record for this book is
available from the British Library

Page design and typesetting by SilverWood Books

For Vanessa, Cleo and Felix

Any fool can paint a picture,
but it takes a wise man to sell it.
Samuel Butler

Contents

Part One

Sales Needs a Rebrand

Chapter 1

Introduction

I believe Sales is long overdue for a rebrand. But how do we as creatives approach that? Often the hardest part of any task we set ourselves is getting started. Where to start? What to do? How to begin? Congratulations on picking up this book. You've now made a start. In some ways, starting to write (or read) this book is much like Sales itself. The hardest part is often just getting going. Usually, once we're there, we quickly forget the initial struggles.

A lot of creative businesses struggle to find consistent sales and growth. They can achieve some short-term wins but then often get distracted whilst delivering those projects, only to find at the end of the process they haven't got any new work. Or, they try to do all of the selling themselves but instead find they get bogged down and distracted by the day-to-day running of their business. Many agencies focus heavily on the creative side and less on the sales side. Creatives, then, have a big problem with growth.

It needn't be like this. There is a new way for new business.

One of my favourite creative quotes is by a famous film director who said: "The hardest part of making a movie is getting out of the car". He's talking about the primal fear he feels when his car pulls up on set and 300 people are waiting for him, his instruction and considerable creative genius, to take control. Perhaps we've all had the 'not wanting to get out of the car moment' from time to time. I know I have and still do occasionally, even now. But get out and begin, we must.

As I sit here, on a plane at 41,000ft (much of this book has in fact been written at high altitude, but more on that later) there are of course several other things I could be doing: reading, working, answering emails, watching a film or – even better – napping! Writing a book about Sales isn't always top of my list when flying. However, much like my work in Sales, it's something I know I need to do and that must be done. Because without sales in my business, in your business, nothing will happen.

So, why have I written this book? Who have I written it for?

There are three main types of people who would benefit from reading this book:

1: Creative Agencies and small businesses in the creative sector

Agency founders and owners

Managing directors or CEOs

Heads of department or senior creative leaders

If you are one of these and either work in or run a creative agency, then there is a lot of information in this book about how to grow your business more effectively. Sales can be a struggle for agencies, and it shouldn't be this way. Most of this book, and the context of the information, has been written specifically for creative agencies.

2: Freelancers and solo creatives who currently earn their living in the industry

Creative directors

Film or art directors

Artists or creative freelancers

The global creative sector is massive. It employs vast numbers of people who earn their living individually – usually through ongoing collaboration with the wider industry. If that's you, then you also will benefit from much of the advice and methods in this book.

3. Start-ups or people wanting to work in the creative industry

Someone starting a new business

Students or undergraduates

Hobbyist creatives

A lot of the content in this book will help you better understand how the creative sector works and how to become more commercially aware with your services or products. It will give you knowledge, tips and tools that you can use either to get started or to gain more work in the industry.

There are other people who may find this book useful or relevant to them from a Sales perspective. Indeed, many of the techniques in this book can be applied to most industries. However, these are the three main audiences and readers who will benefit most from this book.

Sales needs a Rebrand

So, what do I mean by 'Sales needs a Rebrand'? I have slowly come to realise that there is a problem. The problem is so big that it holds back many thousands of people and businesses around the world.

This problem is deeply engrained in our collective thinking. It's a negative viewpoint that is not easy to change or sway. The vast majority of people all think the same way. This creates an obstacle that inhibits most small-to mid-sized businesses and their ability to grow. It's a ball and chain around the ankle. In fact, I would go as far as to say it's the single biggest threat to any small company and its ability to stay in business. And here's the thing: it causes more problems for creatives than anything or anybody else. It makes creative people run a mile and tie themselves in knots. It's a dilemma I see too many creative people wrestle with. It actually jars with them. It's often the opposite of what they think they need.

So then, Sales has an image problem. A major image problem. It's seen as negative when it should be largely a positive force to be celebrated and embraced. As with most public misconceptions, this view on Sales is out of date, largely wrong and quite simply unhelpful. When you add a commercial element does it suddenly invalidate any kind of creative integrity? Of course not.

The UK creative sector is among the best in the world, if not the best. It contributes £13 million every hour to the economy! Our film, fashion, music, arts and creativity are in demand around the world and it is something we really excel at. For more than twenty years I have worked in the creative sector, helping companies grow and sell. I have been incredibly privileged to work with some of the most high-profile businesses, brands, artists and creatives during my career. My work has been with household names – from Abbey Road Studios, EMI Records and lastminute.com all the way through to smaller independent agencies and production companies, selling agency creative work in a variety of specialist areas.

My starting point

I started out at eighteen years old with my first job in the IT industry – selling photocopiers for an office equipment firm. My job was to book appointments for the Sales team to go in and meet clients; in those days, all of which was done over the phone. I was very good at it and broke all the company records. This job ultimately taught me many things: principally, how to sell, how to be highly persuasive, and how to get the required result, all without being overly aggressive, which so many people used to do. Photocopiers and IT equipment are fairly low down the list of priorities for most people. Therefore, I have always maintained – if you can sell this kind of product, you can do anything.

However, there was also a bit of a nagging doubt. Something that didn't quite sit right with what I was doing. Perhaps you could name it a calling. Or a need to scratch a creative itch. I slowly came to realise that I wanted to do something more creative with my life. I began to find my tribe of creatives and colourful characters who were doing interesting things in life and business. I was drawn to the creative industry like a moth to a flame. When I moved to London a whole world and industry began to open up in front of me. I quickly realised this is what I wanted to do.

My first break into a bigger and more exciting industry was actually at the height of the dot-com boom. At twenty-two years old I was part of the commercial team at lastminute.com at the height of the dot-com boom (and then subsequent bust). This was an interesting experience for a young hustler in his first big multinational corporation. It involved working alongside newly household names such as Martha Lane Fox and Brent Hoberman. At this time the world had really never seen anything like it, and everything was changing as the great dot-com tidal wave swept around the world. It was a fascinating place to be and spend a few years working in diverse and fast-moving teams.

From lastminute.com, still keen to do something more creative,

I entered the media and film production worlds, as they were known. Back then 'media' was a catch-all term that seemed to apply to anything broadly creative. I have since worked for large and small creative agencies across most disciplines – film, experiential and events, advertising, digital – both in-house and client-side as new business and sales lead for these agencies.

I have also been fortunate to spend a considerable amount of time in the music industry. Something that part of me still misses to this very day. When you spend your time working with something you truly love it is one of the best feelings in the world. My years in the commercial and Sales teams at Abbey Road Studios and EMI Records were some of the most enjoyable of my career so far. As well as some of the most hedonistic – but that's a story or book for another day!

At the age of thirty I branched out on my own. I was determined to work for myself by this milestone birthday, following the advice from some of my early mentors. In hindsight, I should have done this much earlier but I got there in the end. My advice to anybody thinking of starting out in business on their own is to do it as soon as possible. The sooner you start, the quicker you will be on your own path. Making mistakes, growing, evolving, learning and improving as you go. You might as well do that while you're young to leverage your single biggest asset and advantage: time. Leaving it as late as thirty was fine for me, but earlier is better.

There has never been a better time to start and grow a business. We now have more technology, connectivity and opportunity than ever before. This is a golden age in which to be starting, growing and selling companies. For the last decade I have helped a variety of agency clients, large and small, grow their businesses both in the UK and around the world via my company The Client Key. Representing my agencies, for example on International Government Trade Missions, I've travelled across the globe with no less than two British prime ministers. I've met royalty, from Crown Princes to your regular bog-standard princes (and princesses), sheikhs and sheikhas, presidents, heads of state, captains of industry – the 'who's who' of the UK and global business world.

On many of these trade missions, I've used the trips to actually sell these people some things! You have a very captive audience when sitting on a plane, or travelling between meetings on a minibus, telling mayors, FTSE 100 CEOs and chairmen what you do! I've been lucky to meet global icons and heroes, musicians and rock stars. I've done business (and partied with) some of the most famous people on the planet. It's been a lot of fun!

> **Sales Tip 1: Never miss a Sales opportunity when one comes along!**
> The Client Key helps creative agencies grow: visit us at www.theclientkey.com

On behalf of my clients and agencies I've sold more than thirty million pounds-worth of creative services around the world, which averages out at over one million pounds a year, to date. I've spent two decades honing my craft and practising, refining and developing techniques that help drive revenues and business growth. I've also made many mistakes along the way and had lots of failures. The losses cut deep, and failed pitches are very painful, as any agency head or creative will tell you. Thankfully, there have been far more wins than losses and failures.

All of this combined experience has led me to develop a comprehensive process for effective sales for creatives, creative companies and agencies. In this book I'm going to walk you through it step by step. It is intended as a toolkit that you can use and implement. To understand the process of selling better. To overcome fears, obstacles and problems. Ultimately to help you grow your business.

My work has given me a large degree of success and I've been very fortunate to reap the rewards of a career in Sales. It has also given me the choices that a large degree of financial freedom brings. I've bought, sold and invested in several million pounds-worth of London property. My family and I travel very regularly, and we are incredibly fortunate to live a wonderful lifestyle, all paid for and financed by my career and earnings in selling. Not bad for a lowly salesman who started out selling photocopiers at the age of eighteen!

I am not saying any of this to boast or demonstrate that I have an overinflated ego. No – I am sharing it in order to underline the simple fact that Sales, and selling creativity, has given me an incredibly fortunate and hugely enjoyable life. I'm under no illusion that I am incredibly lucky to do what I do and to reap the considerable rewards. To an extent, I have the ultimate luxury in life: who I choose to work with, when I choose to do it, and how I spend my time. That single biggest thing is the most precious and valuable asset I possess.

So, if I can enjoy all of this success, then why am I writing this book? Why don't more people follow this path and enjoy their own passions and time as they see fit? Well, there is a problem and in fact it's a very, very big problem. The simple fact is that most people dislike selling. Indeed, it actually goes way further than that. The majority of people downright hate it. I have seen people physically recoil at the very mention of the word 'sales'. Some people change colour or break out into a sweat at the thought of having to sell something and engage in the process! Is that you, dear reader? I hope not!

This particular affliction does seem to affect creatives more than most. It is especially noticeable that certain artists or creatives do have an aversion to selling their wares. Perhaps this can be partly explained by the artistic temperament or creative sensitivities. Often, artists are so obsessed with the art of creating, whatever it is they do, that anything else is not considered…or feels of secondary importance. Steve Jobs famously said: "Real artists ship". He was essentially saying that everyone has an idea, but a true artist (or creative) can deliver upon it or ship it. Creativity and ideas can solve many problems and deliver amazing things – but only if you do something with those ideas.

The stigma around selling

So, did you physically recoil when picking up this book? If you did, then fear not. Because we're going to look at some of the reasons why there is such a stigma around 'selling' and what it actually means. Why have we been conditioned to think that way, and is it still a valid viewpoint?

You see, there is a great paradox that we're going to look at more closely throughout this book.

19

And here it is:

> Sales, specifically effective and well-run new business campaigns, are the single biggest thing that a SME creative company can do to grow. It will singlehandedly set you on the path to success if you can find, engage and sell clients your services, repeatedly. And yet, paradoxically, it's the one thing most people hate doing – utter madness!

Why? Because Sales has an image problem. We have been collectively taught and conditioned that selling and salespeople are untrustworthy, and we should be wary. "Never trust a salesman", they say!

Now, this can of course be true and sometimes it is. But my definition of Sales and specifically 'creative selling' is very different from the stereotypical societal view that most of us have been fed for years.

In this book we're going to explore the reasons behind some of this thinking. We're going to understand them more deeply and examine where the negative perceptions originated from. We are going to show you a process and redefine what it means to 'sell' and to successfully grow your business. We're also going to look at how you do that, and explore the most effective ways to get out there and start redefining selling. You can then judge for yourself if Sales is the dirty word it is so often made out to be. There is a comprehensive step-by-step method that is proven to generate business.

So, let's begin. Let's get selling – but not as you think you know it! Before we continue, have you noticed what I have just done in these few paragraphs? I was, of course, qualifying for you my position and authority. Specifically, I was actually qualifying myself and my experience to write this book that you've already spent the last ten minutes reading! I 'sold' just how qualified I am to write this book and what I know about telling *you* how to sell *your* business. Do you now feel that I might have something to say on the business of selling? I hope so!

Never trust a salesperson! Maybe you still think that. Well, perhaps that's about to change.

Let's get started.

> **Sales Tip 2: Qualify.**
> Always qualify your leads, prospects and clients – don't waste your most precious asset and resource (your time) on speaking to people who are not going to buy from you. Always ask yourself why you should spend your valuable time and energy on a prospect. Are they the right person? Will they engage with you? Do they fit your company services? Do they have budget? Can you work with them? If it's a no, then move on. This is what I define as qualifying.

Qualify 'out' as much as you qualify in to get to the right client prospects for your business. Your time is valuable so use it wisely!

Chapter 2

What Sales is not

The great Sales paradox

Many people are averse to the idea of the Sales process. I've seen the discomfort in their eyes and their body language at the very mention of the 'S' word. Could that be you? Or someone you know? A friend, colleague or family member?

People also have differing views on their need or obligations to sell, whether in business or even their personal lives. To a degree, we all need to know how to sell or pitch ourselves. Whether it's for a job interview, a presentation, or just when we meet someone new for the first time. There is an exchange of views, of thoughts and ideas that must be delivered in an engaging way. Therefore, there is an aspect of sales to these experiences.

Yet how often have you heard somebody say that "selling is not for me" or "our business doesn't do selling". I will tell you that I've heard these kinds of phrases said countless times. 'Organic growth' is another line that gets wheeled out very regularly. "We have grown organically," people are proud to say. I suggest that no business will truly thrive on organic growth alone. Someone also needs to facilitate the supposed organic growing sales process because the actual customer transactions won't just happen on their own.

The fear factor runs deep with Sales. It seems to press a deep-rooted physiological warning light that flashes red the moment Sales is mentioned. Why is this? Is it the fact we'll be taken so far out of our comfort zone that we'll be exposed and rejected? Possibly.

Over time, that fear factor has seeped into wider society, and we've collectively been taught to be wary about the act of Sales and selling. We don't think of 'the salesman' as one of the great noble career professions in the same way perhaps that a lawyer or doctor or even a banker is perceived. Academic toil and the world of further and higher education is respected and revered. (Although even bankers are having their own image problems these days. Perhaps they too could also do with some rebranding!)

No. On the whole, the modern salesperson has an image problem. Mention the word 'sales' and we immediately think of shiny suits and door-to-door knocking, or of cold calling (cold calling has quite a lot to answer for with Sale's image problems), and of pushy aggressive, stereotypical young guns eager to make a quick buck at our expense. Or of pyramid schemes, or dodgy financial selling.

Keep your guard up at all times! Never allow these people the time of day, let alone a civilised conversation. Don't answer calls or emails from anyone that remotely displays any of these behavioural traits. They are all bad. They would sell their own grandmother given half the chance and they have nothing to offer me. Furthermore, they want something from me and therefore I must avoid them at all costs.

Sound familiar?

This is how we've been conditioned to behave and be wary of any kind of transactional sale. The idea of being 'sold to' has become problematic and collectively we don't like it.

Quite frankly, who can blame us? If we look at the behavioural traits of some of these aggressive sales industries and tactics, they are deserving of our suspicion and wariness. Our time is precious, and we are naturally defensive when someone attempts to take it from us without invitation. Think of those telephone calls out of the blue. Or unsolicited direct marketing in the post from big brands. These are the tactics that have partly helped give Sales its bad name.

And yet here's the thing...

A truly great salesperson is a magician. They are a master in their ability to conjure up 'something from nothing' in commercial terms at least. They have the power to radically change the course of a company simply through the transactional act of selling something. A great salesperson (and there are millions of them in the world, you just might not have noticed them) is truly one of the greatest assets your company can have. They can grow companies by many multiples – and often in a relatively short space of time. They secure business worth millions of pounds, ensuring companies large and small can employ armies of people in various industries.

Salespeople are the backbone of the modern workforce. Without them no business or organisation can truly thrive, grow and develop at the pace it needs to in today's modern economy. Salespeople are the unsung heroes of today's global economies. And yet on the whole they are still not held in the same high regard as the doctor, the lawyer or our friend the banker. There is still a commonly accepted negative image about the art of selling. There is a huge disconnect between the reality of what Sales is and what it actually means, and also about what it can really do for a company.

There is a paradox in what sales can do, its potential, and what people think of it. Sales, then, has an image problem. Sales needs a Rebrand.

In order to understand why Sales needs a rebrand we first of all have to understand where the problems began. How did we come to think like this? How did this viewpoint of sales in general become widely accepted? Where did some of these bad behaviours originate? Moreover, is our negative perception of Sales still valid today? We need to have a look at where the sales industry has come from. Where did it originate, and what does history tell us? Maybe there are reasons why we've all to come think like this. Or perhaps there are characters who *do* deserve their stereotypical salesman's reputation.

The 1800s – the birth of modern selling

The modern concept of selling, branding and salesmen most likely dates back to the early 1800s. Humans have, of course, been selling, in various guises, for far longer than that and maybe sales really is the world's oldest profession!

In the purest sense, Sales can be defined as the transactional exchange of goods or services. Therefore, Sales as a concept and discipline has been around for as long as we've had goods to exchange. The modern-day notion of what we think of as 'sales' and salesmanship can probably be traced back to the 1800s. Although, as I've acknowledged in broad terms, the notion of selling has been happening for many thousands of years.

America in the 1800s was a time of incredible change and ingenuity. In the mid-1800s the first wave of Chinese immigrants began to arrive in America to work on what was then known as the Pacific Railroad. By 1852 there were 25,000 and by 1880 there were 300,000 Chinese immigrants in America. This huge influx brought with it enormous societal diversion and a potent mix of new people, cultures and products. They brought many traditional medical remedies with them. One of these remedies was snake oil, which for centuries, starting in ancient China, has been heralded as a cure for arthritis and other diseases. Long before it became synonymous with quackery, snake oil was in fact a real medicinal treatment that was hailed as both effective and potent.

Snake oil in its original form did actually have some effect, especially when used to treat arthritis and bursitis. It's very rich in omega-3 fatty acids, which are now known to be potent anti-inflammatory agents. The railroad workers would rub the oil on their joints after a long hard day on the construction site. The story goes that the Chinese workers began sharing the oil with some of their American counterparts, who marvelled at the effects. Snake oil was believed to be so significant and powerful that it quickly caught the attention of the wider American population.

It didn't take long for someone to spot a commercial opportunity in the land of the free. Enter Clark Stanley, a self-described cowboy from Texas. According to the man himself, Stanley had spent many successful years in the Wild West. In 1879, Stanley decided to style himself 'The Rattlesnake King' and began touring America. After his many years working as a cowboy, Stanley claimed to have discovered the powers of snake oil. He understood the recipe, via his time spent with traditional medicine men. Stanley evangelised the powers of snake oil as a cure-all elixir and began selling his product 'Snake Oil Liniment'.

Clark Stanley recounted tales of Hopi 'snake dancers'. He stared deadly rattlesnakes in the face without fear. All this snake-wrangling and cattle-driving solidified his cowboy credentials and he incorporated the elements into an effective sales pitch that supported his brand.

The Wild West had a huge appeal to the American public and Stanley probably had the bravado and charisma needed to sell such lies. He would visit fairs and squeeze live snakes to death in front of his audience. He then plunged their carcasses into boiling water and, when the fat rose, he would use it to make his trademark snake oil on the spot. The public crowded around Stanley's show to catch a glimpse of this flamboyant cowboy and his deadly rattlesnakes. Business was booming. The public, quite literally, couldn't get enough of it.

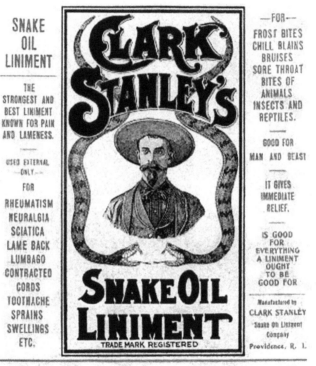

Clark Stanley's Snake Oil Liniment

Is for sale by all druggists. If your druggist fails to have it tell him he can get it for you from any wholesale druggists or it will be sent to you to any part of the United States or Canada upon the receipt of fifty cents in stamps by addressing the

Clark Stanley Snake Oil Liniment Co.

PROVIDENCE, R. I.

While many were impressed, a large number of people thought that Stanley and his oils were bogus. However, it didn't take the general public long to realise that they were being hoodwinked. Many of these supposed 'snake oils' contained alcohol or opium. Most people experienced no real benefits when using the product. A journalist and writer named Samuel Hopkins Adams was a sceptic and sought to out the fraudster. Hopkins Adams carried out an investigation and wrote an exposé revealing the blatant quackery behind Clark Stanley's claims. His piece had testimonies of uncured and duped victims who were injured or became addicted because of Stanley's product. His story *The Great American Fraud* was published in 1905 and a huge public outcry against snake oil followed soon afterwards.

In 1906 the Pure Food and Drug act was passed. Stanley and his claims were subsequently investigated. The snake oil was found to be no more than mineral oil, beef fat, capsaicin and turpentine. It contained not a trace of snake oil. Stanley was fined a fairly paltry $20 for his misdemeanours.

Thus, the term Snake Oil Salesman was born. Clark Stanley took the dubious honour of being the original Snake Oil Salesman.

The snake oil scams left an indelible mark on the psyche of Americans. Since this period the term 'snake oil salesman' has been synonymous with fraud, scams and fakery. We can probably trace the collective wariness in society, and overall pessimism towards salespeople, directly back to 'The Rattlesnake King' – the original snake oil salesman. That term is still widely used today more than 200 years later for dodgy sales practices. It's become a catch-all description for sales scams and dodgy practices. It triggered a behavioural response that is still embodied by many people.

'Snake oil' has had an unfortunate lasting legacy in today's business world. Mr Clark Stanley, cowboy, 'medicine' man, showman and quack certainly has a lot to answer for!

The 20th century

If we think of more modern and negative sales processes, the unpleasant elements of sales, then the used car salesman or door-to-door salesmen spring to mind. In the 1980s, many industries were quickly evolving and maturing. Business had woken up to the need to sell and grow. Retailers, fast-moving consumer goods (FMCG), real estate and many other sectors started to employ armies of salespeople. However, despite all the well-intentioned theory and sales training during all this period of excess, a darker side soon began to emerge.

The double-glazing industry in particular deserves a special mention for their contribution. Well-publicised horror stories began to emerge of salespeople exploiting their customers, principally in the door-to-door sales industries. The consumer magazine *Which?* sent undercover consumers to the leading businesses to find out what was happening: Seven out of eighteen salespeople offered a discount if the undercover researcher signed up immediately; fifteen out of eighteen offered significant savings, often half the original price – the biggest drop was £16,926 from a salesperson representing the best-known double-glazing company of the time. Many of the salespeople offered a lower price with a 'credit deal', but working out how much the customer would ultimately pay was incredibly difficult. One salesperson asked the researcher to sign their name twice to confirm he'd told her the relevant information – a psychological technique to warm up customers.

In all of these worrying examples there is an 'ice to Eskimos' whiff about the sales process. The businesses behind these tactics employed aggressive internal strategies to encourage their teams to sell more. It was a highly competitive environment and teams were incentivised to employ these kinds of tactics. There were big rewards on offer for those that did well. These practices often used a hard sell on vulnerable people to push something they potentially didn't need for capital gain.

The Noughties were when everything changed yet again. Many of us have also been around long enough to fully remember it. Most of us have all played our part in the great tech revolution and embrace the new technologies we have at our disposal. However, in the context of our sales story and history of modern selling, here's where it gets very interesting.

In the Noughties everything suddenly became more sophisticated. The convergence of powerful new technologies and hyper-connectivity brought about new changes and behaviours in a very short space of time. Suddenly the whole world was available at the click of a button through the internet. Social networks have brought instant connectivity and with them a digitally savvy customer base. Here was a way of reaching virtually every customer in the world 'without the need to sell' because the internet would now do that for us. All we would have to do was build it and they would come.

Right?

Wrong.

As the incredible pace of technological innovation played out, the negative sales message and narrative gained yet more traction.

The front-footed sales approach was now very much out of fashion. It was backed up by the widely held belief that the internet would take care of everything. It suddenly became okay not to like, or indeed engage, in direct selling, because here was a (seemingly) perfectly plausible reason not to do it! People suddenly had a brilliant get out clause.

Yes, the internet and social channels have opened up new markets and in ways that were incomprehensible just a few short years ago. The world really is available at the click of a button and, needless to say, it is an essential, critical tool for any business. But, and it's a very big but, it is a complete misnomer that the internet and technology alone will do the sales job for you. It is part of the mix not the complete solution. Too many companies, and a lot of (okay, most!) tech start-ups, overlook this very simple and straightforward fact. There is a view that selling is somewhat out of date and even old-fashioned. I hear this on countless occasions from businesses and often from many tech founders. When I tell them I help companies grow, and sell themselves, I often get a look of slight disdain or sometimes even pity!

The great irony here is that virtually all large Software as a Service (SaaS) businesses employ huge sales teams. They have some of the best and most sophisticated new business teams and processes in the world. This is how they grow. Not by waiting for customers to find them. Or by suddenly 'getting to' $250M in revenues, but by getting out there into the world, connecting with their customers and selling. Companies such as Google, Facebook and Amazon have armies of salespeople. Even aspiring unicorns (the definition of a tech business valued at a billion dollars) will probably have a sales team of at least 100 people. A tech company with $100M revenues (and that is small these days) will easily have fifty people in their sales team. So, why shouldn't smaller companies have them? Because they often have a misguided view that they don't need to sell in the old-fashioned sense.

The balance of power has shifted massively towards the customer and buyer, which in and of itself is a great thing. Suddenly customers – your clients – have more information, more knowledge and more power at their fingertips. They can find you, qualify you, make a quick judgement based on that information (rightly or wrongly) and decide whether to give you any of their most precious resource – their time. Beyond your company website, all of our CVs are now on LinkedIn and all of our personal lives are on Facebook and Instagram. (I often wonder how that has happened or if it's actually a good thing. You can decide for yourself. No matter.) All the potential customer or client has to do is go and have a quick look!

In short, buyers don't need to meet sellers. The old agency world of meet, great, pitch and win has changed, and a lot of people would have you believe that is now the new sales gospel. Underpinned by the great technological safety net.

I am not one of them. I don't believe that this is the new reality for any business or creative agency. Human beings are a social species and we're hardwired to want to interact, communicate and socialise. This is a big advantage for you to leverage in your business.

Whilst a lot of the sales process can now be conducted via technology there will always be a place for a customer interaction at some stage in the process. Buyers want to understand, they want to learn, they want rapport, they want to do their due diligence, and they want a relative degree of certainty in their decision making. Logic makes us think. Emotion makes us act.

Sales Tip 3: What key meetings could you do in person and swap out of a video call?
It is said that only 7% of communication is actually verbal. The rest is non-physical and includes the emotional cues that we pick up when we interact and meet. What more could you learn by being in the room with your clients?

All of this kind of behaviour has been very harmful to sales and its reputation. There is a perception that this is what it means 'to sell'. These practices are unfortunate and damaging. They have no place in today's modern business environment.

We must be clear about what Sales isn't...

Trying to sell them something. Forget that idea for a moment. Instead think about understanding them and their needs first and foremost. Then ask yourself: does it align with us?

Focussing on product not people

Don't forget the golden rule of 'People first. Product second'. Recognise how your clients are approaching any sale and respond primarily to their needs, not yours.

Unprofessional

You always must react appropriately and professionally whatever happens. Not doing so only perpetuates the negative image that we're rebranding.

Confusing people

Keep it simple, especially at first. Don't dumb it down but don't bamboozle people. No jargon. Help make things very simple for them to understand in a short space of time.

Everyone is a prospect

They are not. Qualify and do your homework on prospects. Go after the right people and businesses for you.

Bashing the phones

Contrary to what many people think, the phone is not yet dead. But a more rounded approach to calling is needed. The telephone is still key when used in the right way.

Talking at people

Enough said – listen more than you talk!

Heavy handedness
Bad timing is the death of many a sale. Don't go too hard, too soon, too often – it will have the opposite effect to that intended. You want a lightness of touch as opposed to an over-keen approach.

Scary
The vast majority of clients will be polite and respectful, usually far more than that. Contacting people is okay and should not be feared. They are in business the same way you are. Without selling, having commercial conversations and conducting business activity, none of us would have jobs. Remember that when you're talking to people.

Reading a script
Know what you want to say, but don't stick to a verbatim script whatever you do.

Not being yourself
You do not need to invent some alter ego of who you think the client wants you to be. Be yourself and allow that to come through; people will buy 'you' as much as anything.

Aggressive sales tactics
These never work and are the bad side of selling. Pushing to get deals done inappropriately is a huge NO. You need to have a degree of self-awareness here to realise what is acceptable. If it feels wrong, it almost certainly is.

Tense conversations
Get to a place where you and the client have both relaxed a bit. Lower those tension levels by being yourself; be human.

Not doing your homework
Amateur at best and clients will instantly ignore you. Do the work; find out what you need to know and conduct some research.

Fear of rejection
You will get rejected. Make your peace with it. It's not about you and

it's not personal. Get comfortable with the word 'no'. It's empowering for you and for them.

To be feared

Sales is a game-changer! There are so many reasons why Sales generally has a negative connotation or perception in most people's minds. Some of them, as we've seen, are valid, some of them less so.

For the purposes of growing creative businesses, we should not be afraid of the word sales! It is not a dirty word. It is the lifeblood of any commercial enterprise. Ultimately it is the key to sustaining creative ideas for any agency, artist or individual wishing to earn their living selling creativity.

Chapter 3

What Sales is

We have now looked at the historical problems with Sales. There are many falsehoods behind its image problem and why many people have such a negative view of selling their company and indeed themselves. We've also begun to look at the reasons and needs for doing so.

Now let's start to redefine and clarify what 'Sales' means. Sales needs a Rebrand!

Sales is, in essence, storytelling. For one simple reason above all else: stories build connections. Storytelling is possibly the oldest art form of them all. People have been telling stories quite literally since the beginning of the human race. They started around campfires, possibly the most wonderful kind of storytelling there is. In their influential book *Made To Stick*, Chip and Dan Heath uncovered an amazing statistic: 'After a presentation, 63% of people remember stories. Only 5% remember a statistic.'

People forget facts but they remember stories.

The art of storytelling

When we tell a story (and all of us tell stories) we connect on a personal and emotional level. Truly great storytellers convince people to act – or more specifically in this context, to buy – using trust, emotion and logic. Some of the greatest theological, scientific and philosophical ideas or concepts would not have been established as undisputed fact today without the art of great persuasion (and storytelling) by their proponents.

On 25 May 1961, John F Kennedy announced the goal of landing a man on the Moon in the US Congress. At that point, the total time spent in space by an American was no more than fifteen minutes. In September 1962 Kennedy gave his now infamous speech at Rice

University: "We choose to go to the moon". In this speech Kennedy outlined his vision as space being the new frontier and invoked a pioneer spirit that encapsulated the American way. He suggested a sense of urgency and destiny that inspired many Americans. He was able to pitch the romance, the dream, the common humanity of reaching beyond Earth. Beyond our physical boundaries as human beings and into a new, unknown, realm.

The speech resonated widely and began a new golden era in space exploration. Kennedy articulated a romantic notion of space, one that appealed to citizens – not just of America, but also the wider world.

When Kennedy proposed sending a rocket and a man to the moon, he had to persuade 300 million people to back his big idea. Think about that for a moment. One man, pitching a seemingly impossible, ludicrous, ruinously expensive idea to a nation of 300 million people. And yet, they believed him. More than that, they actively bought into it and became a collective army of champions who endorsed and supported his grand plan. John F Kennedy was able to do this because he was a great visionary and storyteller. He was a genius at selling a big idea.

The Apollo programme captured the nation's attention. It came to symbolise the power and ingenuity of America in a highly competitive race to space with the Soviet Union. His goal of putting a man on the moon was of course achieved, although not until 1969, long after he had died.

Television and the art of modern advertising

In 1927 the invention of television, and subsequent national TV networks, changed everything about the way businesses sold their products. Suddenly, here was a platform for companies and marketers to reach an army of willing consumers across the country. It was a highly potent mix of social change and technological invention all delivered to a ready customer base. Now brands had a voice. They had a platform on which to compete and sell themselves. What they needed was expert help in doing so in creative, engaging and memorable ways.

So began the birth of modern advertising and the birthplace of the traditional 'ad man'. Agencies such as JWT and Young &

Rubicam were already established and growing quickly during this period. These two agencies alone would go on to dominate in later years and are both essentially still in business today.

Many of the advertising greats were cutting their teeth during this time. One in particular is sometimes referred to as the father of modern advertising who went on to establish and run one of the most successful ad agencies the world has ever seen – David Ogilvy.

Born in 1911 in Surrey, England, by the 1930s Ogilvy had already dropped out of Oxford University and been to Paris to work in a 'slavish' hotel kitchen. He described that job as having taught him discipline, management skills and knowing when to move on – three essential qualities when selling anything!

Ogilvy started selling Agas and had the Midas touch. He could quite literally sell to anyone. In fact, he was so good at it that the Aga company asked him to write the sales manual, *The Theory and Practice of Selling the AGA Cooker*. Thirty years later *Fortune* magazine described it as the finest sales manual ever written. So, next time you see a decades-old Aga in an English country cottage, maybe, just maybe, it was sold, and put there, by the great man himself.

I can personally relate to Ogilvy, having also dropped out of university and worked in numerous restaurant kitchens. As I have already mentioned, I also started out my very early Sales career selling photocopiers on the phone and face to face. Both of these jobs required enormous tenacity, resilience and persistence. Let me tell you again that a photocopier is very low down the list of most people's priority in any business! Luckily, you have bucket loads of those things in your twenties. I recognise the conditioning similarities in how Ogilvy ended up becoming such a practised salesman. I very much doubt I'll get the *Fortune* accolade – but hey, you never know.

Sales Tip 4: Tenacity and resilience.
These are essential qualities in Sales. Many people give up after the first attempt in engaging new clients and prospects. It takes a committed, persistent approach. You don't want to annoy people but don't give up – stay the course!

Here is one of the best quotes from Ogilvy's sales guide: "The more prospects you talk to, the more sales you expose yourself to, the more orders you will get. But never mistake quantity of calls for quality of salesmanship."

That's a fantastic way of putting it. What he's essentially saying is this: firstly, you need plenty of conversations, or in other words a decent pipeline to start with. That will ultimately help increase your conversion rate and your sales. However, the quality of those conversations must be high. This is not about vacuous, meaningless connections to make up the numbers. Rather, high-quality, deeply insightful communications and questions with your prospective customers.

Ogilvy's sales approach was rigorous and methodical. He mixed research and intelligence with wit and a unique proposition.

Ogilvy founded the New York-based ad agency Hewitt, Ogilvy, Benson & Mather in 1948 (which later evolved into Ogilvy & Mather Worldwide and latterly just 'Ogilvy'). Supposedly without a single ad penned in his lifetime, but simply a natural talent in sales, he went on to dominate the ad scene in the 50s and 60s. His exhaustive and extensive research methods were unparalleled. Ogilvy was rigorous in his ability to find out everything he could about his customers and to use that knowledge to help him build connections.

Here he is again: "In general, study the methods of your competitors and do the exact opposite. Find out all you can about your prospects before you call on them. Their general living conditions, wealth, profession, hobbies, friends and so on. Every hour spent in this kind of research will help you impress your prospect."

Advertising, to David Ogilvy, was an information medium, not an art form, and demanded rigorous 'homework' before it could gain attention and avoid audience boredom. It had to be supported by disciplined, focussed and consistent concepts. He taught the world a lot and it's worth looking up some of his wise quotes and sayings online as part of your own 'homework'. A business and creative genius, his belief in the power of sales was central to his entire philosophy. Without sales, you have no customers and no business.

The hot-shops

By 1966, the peak of London in the Swinging Sixties, the best creatives were mixing with pop stars, film stars and fashion photographers. They had connections, talent and power that could influence – and sell. A country that was notoriously 'buttoned up' and sensitive to being sold to suddenly engaged and learnt to enjoy these now legendary advertising campaigns.

The newest and most successful agencies in London and New York were called 'hot-shops' and clients flocked to them. As well as Ogilvy, there were other titans such as Bill Bernbach and George Lois – gladiators doing battle on Maddison Avenue and Soho. Their work was innovative and iconic. This was the beginning of a creative revolution. Bill Bernbach, Julian Koenig and Helmut Krone's adverts for Volkswagen and the Beetle were game-changers. They set the course for decades of arresting creative power which continues with the brand to this day.

Selling a quirky small German car (personally commissioned by Hitler, don't forget) so soon after WW2 was about as tough a brief as you can get. It needed a talented creative mind to sell it to American and British consumers. Both their campaigns 'Think Small' and 'Lemon' are widely acknowledged to be some of the greatest advertisements of all time. The brilliance of George Lois can be found in his book *Damn Good Advice (for people with talent!)*. This is a typically arresting headline from a man who made a career of doing so.

In his book, Lois declares that: "creativity can solve almost any problem – the creative act, the defeat of habit by originality, overcomes everything...even a brilliant idea won't sell itself. To sell work I could be proud of, I've had to rant, rave, threaten, shove, push, cajole, persuade, wheedle, exaggerate, flatter, manipulate, be loud and always sell, passionately!"

My own personal favourite campaign of his is the very famous 'Who the hell is Tommy Hilfiger?' It quite literally put him on the map overnight, with the brilliance of advertising creativity and an original idea translating into sales. You often see this advert 'reimagined' (putting it politely) by other creatives even now, decades later.

The TV drama series *Mad Men* immortalised this golden era of advertising and ultimately creative sales. All of the greats from this era had one thing in common: their ability to sell an idea, a story or a product. Here's George Lois again: "Always remember you're trying to sell something. So, ask for the sale!" I'll cover how to ask for the sale in Part Two.

During the 1970s and well into the 1980s British creativity and advertising was gaining recognition as among the best, if not the best, in the world. Names like Sir Frank Lowe, and Maurice and Charles Saatchi began to emerge as the hottest new names in ad land. The Saatchis also had a powerhouse as their financial director during this golden era. A certain Martin Sorrell, later to become Sir Martin.

The Saatchis were so determined to win and succeed that they went to extraordinary lengths within their agency. Their talent, drive, ambition and ability to sell themselves better than anybody else or any other agency quickly stood out. They had a sheer belief that they would win any client, account or pitch – and they usually did.

Another Saatchi alumni, the legendary Tim Bell, reportedly used 'the blink system' when arranging client fees. When a client asked how much, he would, without fail, always reply: "£100k". If the client didn't blink, he'd say: "A month".

The Saatchis combination of creativity, perceived political-insider status, and unquestionable business success was irresistible. Suddenly Saatchi & Saatchi were talked about in the same way as great American companies such as JP Morgan and IBM. They were both revered and feared in equal measure. They had power and influence, and they were deserving of their reputation. Saatchi & Saatchi became the 'go to' international advertising agency virtually overnight.

These were all great salespeople, in their ability to bring their ideas and perspectives to the world. They understood the power of storytelling, of evidence and fact. They were able to combine all of these into logical, powerful and emotively persuasive arguments. They were able to effectively sell their ideas to the world.

So, perhaps when you next catch yourself thinking sales is bad – remember great salespeople are in very good company. Any fool can paint a picture, but it takes a wise man to sell it.

Let's now be very clear about what the art of Sales is...

You can think of what follows as a set of themes and guiding principles in all of your new business and sales conversations. They can serve as a reference to use as you develop and begin. These are a set of easy guidelines to help us start to break down the sales process into bite-sized chunks:

Listening

The first rule of law in Sales. Listen more than you talk. Practise becoming a better listener. Most people listen with the intent to respond, planning their response. Instead, try to be an active listener. Asking questions will allow you to understand more. Also think about what's *not* being said, as this can often be just as revealing as what *is* being said. I could write a whole book on listening, but the main principle is: if you do one thing, talk less – listen more!

Understanding people

First and foremost, you are simply trying to understand the other person or company. Not trying just to sell them something – that can come (fairly naturally) later. Once you've understood a little more about that person you can begin to understand their needs and work out whether they align with yours.

Open questions

To listen you need to understand. To understand you need to ask lots of questions. Open questions are designed to get the other person talking. Think 'what' and 'how' in front of any question and you will get them talking so that you can listen.

Helping people to buy

Selling is about helping people to buy. It's a simple idea but it should govern everything you do. Move away from the traditional notion of 'selling' and help them understand you, your business and your value. The sales part will inevitably take care of itself.

Learning

Listening and understanding will help you to learn more about your clients and their business. Learn as much as you can and use that knowledge. Go the extra mile and find that nugget of information that will make the difference. If you don't, somebody else, probably your competitors, will.

Building rapport

It's your job to help lower the tension levels in any conversation as quickly as possible. Both you and your client will have a degree of tension in any first conversation or meeting. It's hardwired into our DNA as human beings to be a little wary in unfamiliar situations. Use the above tools to lower the tension levels and build rapport. Just a little: aim for the appropriate amount of rapport and no over-familiarity too soon.

Thinking like your clients

Put yourself in the mind of your clients and try to walk a mile in their shoes. Why should they talk to you? How are you relevant? See things from their side of the fence. Try to think like a client when pitching. Consider how you will be perceived in their mind. Also, recognise their time pressures – if you can tell someone is busy then arrange to speak another time.

Timing

Finding the right balance when contacting clients is key. Three to four weeks in real life actually feels like just one to two weeks to a client, especially when you don't know them that well and they're still a prospect. Remember this as a general rule: don't be tempted to follow up every five minutes. You have to sense when the right time is to call, email, meet or follow up. Your instincts and intuition will play a key part here and you'll learn not to go too soon, or too late. Timing can make all the difference between a 'yes', or a 'no'.

Thinking creatively

Knowing how and when to get in touch with someone and land the right message takes some thought. Think in their mindset about would work and what wouldn't. Some creative thinking is called for, and don't be tempted to just fire stuff out and hope for the best. Make it different and memorable, and get clever as to how to contact people.

A holistic approach

There is no one-size-fits-all approach to selling your company. You have to try things and experiment. Take a 360-degree view to the various tools you can deploy. Simply doing some lead generation, email marketing or event networking in isolation won't work. Take a broad view and work through a holistic plan.

Consistency

Keep the sales rhythm and pulse going once you've started it. It can be so tempting to take your foot off the gas once in a while. Especially on the back of a win or some success. Don't do it. Ever! It will be especially hard to get back to where you were in the first place and a challenge to make up any lost ground. Keep going!

Credibility

Whatever you do, make sure it's credible. Ask yourself, and your team, is it good enough? Would I buy it as a client? Occasionally the answer will be 'no', and you might have to ruffle a few feathers internally. Integrity should run through every conversation, contact and connection with the client. The minute you lose integrity, clients will always pick up on it and you've lost credibility.

Critical to your business

Sales is as important to your business as the creative department (or whatever service line your business is) and your finance dept. More so, in fact! Embed the commercial sales function at the heart of the business. Bake it in – put it front and centre. Now! It should be *the* single most important thing in your business. Nothing will happen until someone (probably you) sells something.

Making things happen

Effective sales are transformative and a game-changer. It gives you the framework to get out there and make stuff happen. Be deliberate about what you do and be the one controlling the narrative for your company. Don't be the person who wonders: "What just happened?"

Closing

Many people get stuck here, as their inherent politeness kicks in and they fall at the final hurdle. Don't be afraid to ask clients how to proceed and win the business. They will expect you to do it – and it's your job to do it!

Communication

Most great salespeople are good communicators. Being very clear with your messaging and content will help things land quicker. Also, make sure you communicate internally, too. Sales is a team sport so make sure you've got the players you need, in the right positions, and they're all talking to each other on a regular basis.

Qualifying

Your time is your most valuable asset and resource. It is just as valuable as a client's time, more so in fact. Make sure you qualify your clients 'in' or 'out'. Are they a viable prospect for you? Should you invest your time in them? If not, move on and find the ones where you should invest. Don't get caught in the trap of wasting time by not qualifying people.

Persistence

There will be times when you lose clients, or you lose a pitch. It's just a fact of life and the nature of business. It will hurt a lot and it's a terrible feeling. But you have to learn from it. Ask for feedback, question what happened, analyse and then move on. Whatever you do, don't give up. Stay in the game.

Belief

When you go into a conversation have full belief in yourself, your idea or your company. If you don't have that belief, ask yourself: what is not right? Trust me, clients will spot the lack of belief a mile off. Conversely, when you're fully on board, and have 100% belief in what you're saying, you will ooze knowledge, authority and confidence that clients will find very hard to resist.

Fun

Sales is fun or at least it should be. Try to find the bits that you enjoy and celebrate your successes. Laugh at your failures. We're not trying to put a man on the moon; we're just trying to talk to some people and understand them. At its heart, Sales is a very human and social activity. Have some fun whilst you're doing it!

Empowering

An effective sales strategy will help give you the power and tools you need to grow your business. That in turn will give you choice: on the companies you work with, the people you employ, the work you produce, the money you generate and the life that you live. Ultimately, what could be more empowering than that?

We have begun to look at why Sales has a negative reputation, and why it needs a rebrand. Now we need to look at what Sales really is, how we redefine it and how you can learn to implement it in your business. How it can serve you – the creative – to grow and flourish in your business.

The creative industry was born on an ability to sell. It would not have become what it is without that underlying principle. Over time, we have lost some of that thinking. It has become clouded in the messages that Sales is negative.

Before we look at what Sales *is*, and to help you finally reframe and dispel some of those negative images, let's have a look at some of the world's best salespeople.

The best salespeople...are not salespeople!

Some of the most high-profile people in the world are masters at the art of selling. They understand the inherent value in their products and have a natural ability to connect those products to customers. This is not an easy thing to do. These people are not often thought of as salespeople and perhaps you have never considered them in this way, either. You only have to look around you to find great examples of people who have this natural talent.

Here are a few of my favourite examples:

Steve Jobs

There's been at least one book written about his brilliance at presentations, and there have been studies on his skills as a communicator. However, very few people talk about him as a salesman, which was one of his many skills.

Throughout his life, Steve Jobs was a fascinating, contrary and brilliant salesman. He had the ability to call anyone, reach anyone, and assert the power of his personality to ensure he got the result he wanted. He was driven, self-centred and unrelentingly focussed. He was a master at spotting the gap and opportunity for his products. His presentations (an artform in themselves) always explained the 'why' before the 'how'.

Not many people will recall the storage of an original iPod (5GB), but they might remember it was suddenly possible to carry a thousand songs in your pocket. It became an instant headline and hit around the world. Steve Jobs was a master at bringing products into the spotlight and creating a need. He operated at the nexus of creativity and innovation – and had a complete mastery of the art of sales.

Oprah Winfrey

Oprah Winfrey is one of the world's great salespeople. She has created an incredible legacy that will be remembered and studied long after she's gone. This is a woman who is a billionaire (several times over) and yet incredibly she doesn't make a single physical product! She has built her fortune on selling the one thing she knows best – herself. Oprah's product is her and her personal brand. How has she done it?

Oprah is selling to you – you just don't usually notice. She's selling an aspiration, a lifestyle and an opinion you can trust. Since her launch in 1986 she now owns and operates OWN (The Oprah Winfrey Network), *O – The Oprah Magazine*, and Harpo Productions (her name spelled backwards). Dubbed the 'Queen of All Media', she was the richest African American of the 20th century and she has often been ranked the greatest black philanthropist in American history.

Oprah has that deft touch that all truly great salespeople have – an ability to connect with others in a genuine way. By opening herself up and facing some deep and intimate details such as her weight problems, tumultuous love life, and sexual abuse, and by crying alongside her guests, she has been credited by *Time* magazine with creating a new form of media communication known as 'rapport talk' and 'Oprahfication', as *The Wall St Journal* termed her style. Oprah Winfrey is a global icon. She is the ultimate saleswoman and one of the most successful salespeople on the planet.

Banksy

Banksy is possibly one of the best examples of selling creativity. He has created an aura and mystique around both his identity and his art. He understands the sales process better than virtually any other living artist. Yet he's revered as one of the world's greatest artists. This is how we collectively see him.

He's able to generate such interest in literally anything he does that the commercial side, or sales, is simply a forgone conclusion. He is oversubscribed many times over. All copyright and identity claims and certificates of authentication are tightly controlled by the best lawyers in the business. He employs armies of them. I know this because I've had to deal with them to authenticate two prints I used to own!

Banksy has the art world and general public eating out of his hand whenever he decides or chooses. He is the absolute embodiment of the artistic sales process.

Damien Hirst

Hirst is another artist on the UK rich list. With an estimated net worth of approximately $500 million, Damian Hirst is one of the world's best-selling artists. His shows sell out months, even years, in advance and he is as controversial as he is successful.

In 2008 he broke the record for a single artist auction 'Beautiful Inside My Head Forever', which generated sales of nearly $200 million. This was an unprecedented result for an artist at a time when global markets were crashing and in crisis. Think what you like about the overt commercialisation of his art but there is no denying his success or his ability to sell.

Sir Richard Branson

Is there anyone better at generating column inches or coverage than Sir Richard? He has built a career (and multi-billion-pound fortune) on a knack of knowing how to publicise himself, and therefore sell.

In the 80s and 90s I grew up watching Branson race across oceans, fly around the globe in hot-air balloons and build a world-famous airline. He also ran one of the biggest and most successful record labels and signed some of the most famous artists in the world. All of these things he did with flare and talent. He is the ultimate frontman in business, with an army of talented people operating behind him to deliver and help make his vision a reality. These days he's about to start flying people into space via his new Virgin Galactic brand.

Sir Richard Branson holds the view that nothing in life can represent total failure. He is not afraid to try, experiment and show up. In his words: "Screw it, let's do it".

Greta Thunberg

Greta Thunberg is a master salesperson. Although she's mostly referred to as an activist. Is that just another name for a proactive salesperson?

She has single-handily garnered the collective voice of several generations across the most important issue of our time. She speaks directly and bluntly and is not afraid to criticise. Part of her success in communicating, and in making an impact, is that she focusses on a single clear message. She employs storytelling techniques that use heroes, villains and plots to rally support. At the time of writing, she is not even twenty years old! You could learn a lot about selling just by watching Greta.

Look around you. Great salespeople are everywhere you look, if you start to notice them. In your office. Part of your family. In the news and media. These are the people who can articulate ideas. Who can persuade and cajole, with passion, charm and flair! The greatest salespeople are not always thought of as salespeople!

The single biggest thing you can do – the game-changer

In its purest sense, the art of Sales and selling creativity is quite simply about making things happen. Specifically, making them happen for your business. As we've now seen above, some of the greatest businesspeople in the world understand this simple fact better than most: without Sales nothing happens. No growth, no customers, no choices, no options. And options are what you need in business to withstand the continuing and unrelenting pressure. The great Lord Sugar described business as being about one thing: pressure. I think he's absolutely right.

In order to grow your business, you have to be able to find a way to implement a clear strategy for understanding who your potential clients are and converting them, via an effective sales process, to become customers. It is the single biggest thing you can do to grow your company.

Most of the great sales and businesspeople I know all share a common trait in their ability to make things happen. There are, I suggest, generally three types of people in the world:

- The people who make things happen.
- People who let things happen.
- Those who wonder what the fu*k just happened?

Read that again and consider which one you are. Do you let things happen, or make things happen?

Generally, I prefer to try and stay in the first category. Especially when I'm engaged in growing businesses that I run, or for our clients. An ability to engineer a result and find a way to cut through is so important in succeeding with new business. I sometimes do find myself in the last two categories. Things don't always go to plan and I'm only human like the rest of us. On occasion the best option is to just let things happen and the right answer will usually reveal itself. But generally, I always try and stay in the first category.

Personally, having the drive and restless energy to get things done has always come naturally to me. Perhaps that's why I've been successful in Sales and in my business. I don't claim to be a superhuman multitasker, able to get endless to-do lists ticked off (not that's really a good idea either) but I am what you might call a 'do-er'. Understanding what is going to make the difference to my business and my clients' businesses and not getting too distracted from that focus. Knowing what is going to make the fastest impact and then delivering it is critical.

However, Sales does not always come naturally to many people. Possibly the vast majority of people in fact. There can be people who put off the doing, or worse never get started at all. But if you don't sell then you don't grow. If you don't grow then your business will either bump along the bottom or, worse, die. Thus in 'brutally simple' terms (borrowed from the Saatchis) we must grow or die.

We now live in a hyper-competitive world and business marketplace. Clients have more information and more knowledge at their disposal than ever before. Luckily, so do you! Seemingly, they have more control and power. The balance has tipped in their favour. Luckily, so do you! You have the same amount of information at *your* fingertips to know what you need to do – it's a question of doing it.

Making the time is the first step in getting things done. Carve it out. Do whatever's required to find the time. Most people claim to be too busy and time poor. Unfortunately, nothing is going to happen until you liberate yourself to find time and take action. Begging, borrowing or stealing it – but making the time. We will look at some effective ways of time management and getting sales stuff done in Part Two.

Sales Tip 5: GSD – Get Sh*t Done!
Do It! or Ditch It is the title of a great book by Bev James on the subject of getting things done. Do it or ditch it speaks for itself. What can you ditch and what do you need to get done? How is your inbox management? To quote the late Donald Rumsfeld: "If you're constantly working at the top of your inbox, you are working on other people's priorities".

Sales and selling should not be an impossible task. You understand your business better than anyone. Therefore, it should be easy for you to understand your clients better, too. It will take some practise and it undoubtedly will take effort. Tell me about a new skill that doesn't! Like any skill, it must be learnt, practised and hopefully, mastered.

Learning the art of Sales can be simplified as learning to understand people better. In this case, a specific category of people: your clients. Understanding this simple idea is one way you can get over the sales hump which you may be experiencing.

Rather than seeing it as you must sell someone something, try reframing the narrative that you are simply trying to understand them. Because once you understand them, then you will understand their needs. Once you know their needs you can take a view if they align with your business and progress the conversation.

> **Sales Tip 6: Framing, positioning and timing are art forms.**
> Think about how you frame your key messages to make them clearer and easier to understand. Timing is also crucial.

Whilst writing today, I have just secured a film interview with one of the country's best known and high-profile businesspeople on behalf of a client I work with. He had never heard of me, nor met me, before I contacted him, but I framed my email in such a way that I thought would appeal to him. I also knew that by waiting a week to follow up, and not pursuing it too quickly, I stood more of a chance of him saying 'yes' to the interview. Which he did!

Think about slowing down when you follow things up; you don't always need to rush.

When done properly, Sales is truly a game-changer. It injects an energy and momentum into any business (especially creative ones) that is transformative. Best of all, it will feel great doing it. When things start to click, you get into a sales rhythm and a state of natural flow. It's one of the most satisfying, rewarding things you can experience in your business. It will elevate your organisation to a higher level than you would have thought possible.

Sales is the true lifeblood of any company and yet many people have the view that 'sales' is negative. A dirty word even. How crazy is that!

So, Sales needs a Rebrand. We need to reframe our view of what Sales is and unleash its full potential for the benefit of your business.

Part Two

The Creative Sale: Process

Chapter 4

Getting started

By now I hope you're starting to feel more comfortable with the idea of sales. Maybe you are even looking forward to getting started and selling? In order to do that, it's important to have a very clear process, and structure, to any sales campaign. What's the best way to get started? How should you approach things for your business? What are the key areas to cover and in what order?

Unfortunately, there is no magic bullet or singular solution that can be deployed to short- cut your success. Anybody that tells you otherwise is talking rubbish. However, the art of Sales (and selling) is a skill that can be practised and learnt. It's a money-making growth tool – a knack and 'superpower' that you can acquire.

As we've already seen, clearly, there is a right and wrong way to go about things. We certainly do not aspire to be Mr Clark Stanley or indeed an archetypal 80s salesman. Rather, we aspire to be the calm, assured confidence and knowledgeable authority of Mr David Ogilvy in his glorious 1960s heyday. Therefore, we must have a plan and we must stick to it.

Luckily, Sales is a subject that most people have already had some experience with. Many of us are selling anyway in our day-to-day lives, although we perhaps don't realise it. We're listening and engaging with our colleagues, offering support to friends, negotiating with our kids, persuading or communicating. All of these things are everyday examples of behavioural 'selling'. Most of them we do unconsciously without having to think too hard about it. With our renewed sales focus we need to use the skills we already have (everyone is able to listen and communicate – to a point!) and bring them to fore in a new way. We need to focus on the conscious competence matrix, which is shown on the next page.

That's our starting point, a conscious competence platform upon which you can build. It's a teachable skill that can be learnt. In this

UNCONSCIOUS INCOMPETENCE	UNCONSCIOUS COMPETENCE
You are unaware of the key skill and your lack of proficiency	Performing the skill becomes second nature
CONSCIOUS INCOMPETENCE	CONSCIOUS COMPETENCE
You are aware of the required skill but not yet proficient	You are able to use the skill, but only with effort

section of the book, I'm going to share a framework and process that you can directly implement into your business. It's tried, tested and proven and I guarantee you that it will get results if followed in the right way.

There are three core components to building and delivering effective sales campaigns within creative businesses (this also applies to most other types of company, too).

These components are:

• Finding clients
• Engaging clients
• Winning clients

The following sections of this book will guide you through each of these core components in detail. They are designed to be a step-by-step guide that you can use and implement within your business. It's a sales methodology that has generated millions of pounds, not just for me but for my clients and their businesses. My method is tried, tested and proven. You can refer back to each step as a framework and structure as you go, and it's intended to guide you as you build your sales function.

If you're working on your own as a sole trader, then you might choose to implement this method on a week-by-week basis – but you should implement it as quickly as you can! If you have the luxury of a team (lucky you) then the method can become the backbone of your sales team and will help guide your energy and efforts. Start using it as a tool that you all engage with and own.

Delegate parts of the method if you like, but don't let them slip through the net at any cost. All of the parts of this process are important. Hold your team accountable. Hold yourself accountable! Be honest about what's being done, your progress and where you're falling short. Rigorous honesty, ownership and accountability around these sales steps is essential to your success.

Time management

Before we get into the detail and methodology, this is a good moment to mention time management. Time is the biggest enemy of any sales campaign or project. It is usually the most common reason that people give as to why things are not working: "I just don't have the time".

In order to successfully grow and sell your business we must understand how time (or lack of it) can be a barrier to overcome. There is always something else you could be doing. If you're someone that has shied away from selling within your business, I'll bet you're often finding a way to put this off...

Well, no more!

In order to get started you have to *make* the time. Sales has just come front and centre. It's your top priority. We're looking for a consistent approach, not one full day and then forgetting about it until next month.

Let's get these principles entrenched:

• Regularity
• Frequency
• Consistency

Little and often is best to start with. I would advocate setting yourself small and achievable goals. Don't make the (very common) mistake of setting unrealistic expectations. That's why so many people fail at diets. For example, they say: "I'm not going to eat *any* carbs, sugar, chocolate or ice cream for three months" instead of saying something like: "I'm not going to eat sugar, chocolate or ice cream for a week – but I'll allow myself some carbs this weekend".

If you don't keep your goals right-sized then you just set yourself up to fail. Think honestly about what's stretching but achievable for you. You can always revise your goals or KPIs (Key Performance Indicators) and make them more challenging as you go. However, to begin with, make them bite-sized, realistic and deliverable. It feels much better when you start achieving them, and achievement will increase motivation.

It's vital to carve out the time to make all of this happen so that it becomes a reality. The world is full of distractions. Smartphones in particular, whilst they are an amazing tool, have a lot to answer for in terms of our reduced attention span and productivity. They are a big enemy of effective sales. They are a huge distraction and often a barrier to success. Make them work for you and not the other way around.

Sales Tip 7: Own your phone.
Use your phone in the right way. Don't let it rule you (as most people do), especially when you're trying to focus on sales and clients. Put it in another room. Turn off the screen notifications (a game-changer). Put it in airplane mode. Put it in a cupboard. Use a landline or video call.

Put the caller announcement on so it tells you who's ringing from the other side of the room, then ask yourself – do you really need to speak to your partner or your best friend at 11am on a Tuesday morning when you're halfway through some sales work? No, focus on the task in hand and give it your entire attention and energy. Throw the phone out of the window, if you must. Do whatever you need to do to stop it distracting you. It's a plague of the modern world and it gets in the way.

By adding in the good things, slowly, you'll eventually 'crowd out' some of the bad habits. Over time this rule of 'add in' and 'crowd out' becomes a really effective way of making progress. It gets you into a rhythm. It will help implement long-lasting behaviour change.

> **Sales Tip 8: 'Add in' and 'crowd out'.**
> Think of the rule as 'add in and crowd out'. This rule has many applications but it's particularly important when forming new habits. 'Add in' an hour of sales activity a day and do it for a week. Then 'add in' half an hour's calling, say two weeks later.

Overall, it's essential to make a start. I cannot repeat this enough. Getting started is often the hardest part to do overall. Remember that famous film director and what he said about getting out of the car? That primal fear he felt? Getting started can be intimidating. The fear factor kicks in. But you've got to stare fear straight in the face and say: "Out of the way...let's go" and just get out of the car.

This process is designed to give you structure and clarity once you've begun; to help keep you focussed and stay in a successful rhythm.

Sales is not a dirty word and nor is it a dirty business. It's a tool that will help you get paid more for your ideas, your creativity and your true value.

So, let's get going and let's get selling!

Chapter 5

Sales plan and strategy

A sales plan and strategy is essential for you as you make a start in growing your business. Ultimately the aim is to hold yourself to account on strategic planning. Your business needs a clearly defined vision as to how it will sell, grow and attract new clients. By setting a course and sticking to it, your chances of success will improve dramatically. It is vital that you – as the business leader, senior salesperson, or key individual – adhere to this plan.

To use a pertinent and popular saying: "Don't get stressed, get a plan" (and stick to it!).

This is your opportunity to set the course for your company and for you to decide how it will grow. Start by clarifying your end goal. It might seem counter-intuitive to begin at the end, but it's a great way of understanding your aims and objectives. Perhaps you might want to double your turnover. Or possibly add three new clients in a given time period, say six to nine months. Whatever you are looking to achieve in your business, it's important to crystallise those aims and establish your vision for the company. Setting a goal is the first step to any effective sales and new business campaign.

Fortunately, this sales plan does not need to be a long and extensive document. In fact, I would recommend that it is relatively short and concise. The more succinct and goal-orientated, the better. It will allow you, and your team, to stay fully focussed on the job in hand, and on delivering it. I sometimes see people tripping themselves up because they are not clear and concise about the objectives, aims and expected outcomes. To a certain extent, less is more here. Remember, this is purely about growth and sales – not operational or delivery elements of the business. That's a separate conversation (and a separate plan). Of course, you may want to factor in or be aware of any demands in those areas but stay focussed on the goal.

A strategy is essential to guide you through the process of your whole sales campaign. Without a clear plan you run the risk of not staying focussed on your objectives and aims.

Ten key questions

In order to devise a strategy, ask yourself the following *ten key questions:*

1. What am I trying to achieve – what outcomes do I want?
2. How will I do this?
3. What are the challenges I must overcome?
4. How can I improve my chances of success?
5. What are my KPIs – are they realistic?
6. What is my time frame?
7. How much time will I (or my team) devote to this?
8. What does success look like?
9. How will I communicate this to my team?
10. How will I learn and get feedback – from my team/clients?

Once you have the answers to these ten key questions, a picture should begin to emerge. This emerging picture is the blueprint for your business and how it will grow. Furthermore, it's totally unique to you and your company. The advantage of working like this and answering these questions is that it is has been customised to help you deliver what you need for your business.

The answers to these ten key questions will help you shape an effective sales plan. You don't need to write *War and Peace*. Sometimes a one-pager is enough. Or perhaps a short presentation or slide deck. But you must communicate very clearly what your aims and objectives are. Be rigorously honest with yourself in terms of goal-setting and the realistic chances of delivering upon them. Remember it's better to keep the goals right-sized and hit them, as opposed to trying to do too much in one go. It will only demoralise you if you do this. Better to start small and grow your ambitions and goals. The sales plan can be reviewed and periodically checked – I would say on at least a monthly basis. It would be an advantage if you have someone that can help provide some accountability. If you're working independently, perhaps an associate or business contact, or even a friend or relative. If you're working as part of a team then find someone who can help, such as a colleague, board member or non-exec. These people can you help you look at things objectively. They won't be as close to any frontline activity as you are, so they will see things differently and give you a fresh and valuable perspective.

Tracking progress

You will also need a method to track and record progress as you go. That means a Customer Relations Management system or CRM. A CRM can take many forms but is a critical tool that you must implement. There are many options and a huge range of different software so take the time to look at the right one for your business. The cost and sophistication will vary.

You may not need a state-of-the-art system that costs thousands of pounds per year. In its most basic form, a CRM can consist of an Excel sheet, Google doc or even a Word doc with your client notes. Perhaps that's a good way for you to get started initially. However you do it, you must track, record and capture your data as you go. But make sure the system you choose is intuitive, cost-effective and – above all – it works for you, because it's an essential tool in your sales process. Sitting there doing one or two hours of data entry each day will quickly get boring and you're likely to give up, so find a CRM that takes a few moments to click, update and type a few notes then set a reminder.

Don't let the CRM data entry tasks become bigger than the client conversations and sales activities! That is not using your time effectively nor is it selling!

So, you have written your strategy and sales plan. Well done on getting this far; most people never do! Now, how can you now ensure it's delivered upon? What is needed to keep it alive and front of mind?

As you might expect, regularity is the key here. In the same way that you will be checking in with your team, advisors or accountability partners on a regular basis, you'll want to do the same with your strategy. In fact, your sales planning and strategy should essentially be the cornerstone of those weekly/monthly conversations. Have regular reviews of your strategy to keep it front and centre of mind – for you, and for everyone on your team.

I'll talk more about how to structure team catch ups in Part Three.

> **Sales Tip 9: Update your data.**
> A CRM is only as good as the data it contains. Put junk in – get junk out! Therefore, if you don't take (or make) the time to keep your CRM updated it's a meaningless tool. The key is to find a system or solution that is manageable and straightforward to you.

Your brand proposition

These days, almost every business operates in a crowded and competitive landscape. This is particularly true in the creative sector and for most agencies. In your particular field alone (whether film, events, design, digital or marketing) there are hundreds if not thousands of competitive companies trying to win your clients – so, when you're pitching for work, you need a clear brand proposition to help your potential clients choose you over your competitors.

Some people will tell you that a unique brand proposition alone will win you clients. It's a nice idea but I don't believe that, on its own, a unique brand proposition will help you win more business or grow your company to any meaningful size. Yes, it might happen from time to time but it is increasingly rare. There is simply too much competition in today's business market, especially the creative agency landscape, for that single thing to grow your company.

On its own, a unique brand proposition is not enough to get the job done. Clients are duty bound and obligated to carry out rigorous pitch processes and follow due diligence when buying projects of any substantial value. Therefore, being able to go through that competitive sales process (which is essentially what a pitch is) better than anyone else will give you a massive head start. It will help you win more business. When you've won the client, built the relationship, and they understand your true value, you may then start to win business without needing to pitch – and that's the point at which your brand proposition can work on its own, but not before.

What's *your* brand proposition? How are you going to effectively gain an advantage over the competition? How will you differentiate your brand, and shine a light on the work your business does? Or more specifically, how can you demonstrate the value you offer your clients – why should they come to you and nobody else?

You could think of your brand proposition as your 'north star' or your 'true north'. It should help guide your day-to-day, month-by-month progress. It's a great anchor to come back to and you can build your whole business around a simple statement. In the creative agency space, my personal favourite is Saatchi & Saatchi's 'Brutal Simplicity of Thought'. Or Landor's 'Extraordinary brand transformation, by design'. There are many other great propositions out there – the trick is to start noticing them and considering how and why they work. Can you use this analysis to form your own brand proposition?

> **Sales Tip 10: Study other brands.**
> Start to notice what great brands are doing with their messages and copy. Good (and bad) copy-writing and communications is all around us. Everywhere. Look out for the ones that resonate and the ones that are average. What can you learn from them? It will help you think about your brand in new and innovative ways.

When combined with an effective sales strategy, your unique brand proposition can be brutally effective. It's a potent combination that will light a fire under your business and really rocket your business to the next level.

Chapter 6

Finding clients

Finding clients is, in many ways, the base camp of any sales strategy. Knowing who you want to approach, and who you'd like to work with, is a basic starting point. However, there is more to it than that and you'll want to invest time in establishing the foundations of your sales strategy and plan. My approach is to take the time to properly consider who your current clients are. This will help you identify your future and prospective clients (your target clients).

Ask yourself some key questions:

- Why do your current clients work with you?
- What business sectors or creative areas are you strong in?
- Where are you weak?
- How do you align to your clients' goals?

When you've answered these key questions, you can begin compiling a measurable metric – your target client list. A target client list will allow you to focus on the prospective clients that are right for you and for your business. This list will be specific and focussed – not generalised, which is a common mistake creatives make.

It's better to start with a long list of target clients and then whittle that down to a short list. You can always come back to some of those companies that didn't make the short list at a later date, but at this stage: be focussed. Think about where you can achieve the quick wins and the 'low-hanging fruit'. Yes, you might want to work with Google or Nike but, actually, how realistic is that in the short term? Would you be better off focussing on more accessible businesses or challenger brands? You want the clients that are going to give you the fastest impact for your business.

> **Sales Tip 11: Go under the radar.**
> Look for the hidden gems. The global behemoths that are under
> the radar. Find the businesses that nobody has heard of but
> are multi-billion-dollar entities. Everyone is trying to work with
> Apple. Who's trying to work with their chip manufacturer? Or their
> packaging manufacturer? Or their architects? Far fewer companies.

Focus on finding those 'under the radar' companies that still need to communicate and market themselves. They are out there and there are lots of them! I've worked with many of these kinds of companies, and they always surprise me both in their size and their low profile, and this has the added benefit of fewer people (your competitors) knocking on their door. Go against the grain slightly here.

Generate a few wins and some successes with these under-the-radar companies, which will in turn allow you to start focussing on the bigger clients. You'll have confidence in what you're doing – success really does breed success – so go for the clients that you know you can win. Work up to the bigger, more ambitious, clients over time. It becomes a virtuous circle and it's addictive once you really get into your flow!

So, now you have your focussed short list, you can begin your research. Research is key to finding those under-the-radar companies and uncovering them. Bring them on to your radar! There is of course a myriad of ways that you can find out the detail. You have a wealth of tools at your disposal, so use them: LinkedIn, company websites, annual reports, social media and the news. Reading the business press is also a great habit to get into. Most people don't do it but even a quick cursory look over the business section of your news feeds and channels will give you ideas, and a basic overview of the client landscape.

Doing your homework at this stage will pay dividends later on, because your alignment with your clients will be better. Your approach, general marketing, comms and sales messages will all be received in a greater way by your prospects if you've actually thought about and researched them.

The shorthand for this process is *Qualifying*.

Qualifying

Qualifying is essential in any sales activity for one simple factor: time. Your clients are qualifying you simply because they don't have much time and they don't want to waste it on you being a potential mistake. So, they qualify you! They'll google you, research you and check you out, at least a little bit. Well, guess what? Your time is just as important as theirs – if not more so. Therefore, you should be doing the same to them. You are looking to qualify people 'out' as much as you qualify people 'in'.

What do I mean by this?

Well, ask yourself whether the target client is a good match or fit for you and your business. Do they really have the budget? Is there chemistry or rapport there? Will they talk to you and engage? If the answer is 'no', then perhaps they are not a good prospect and maybe they should be qualified 'out'.

Saying 'no' and having the confidence to know when clients are not right for you is extremely empowering. With a bit of practice, it can become an automatic sense that you rely on. The quicker you decide on the target clients that are not right, the faster you'll get to the ones that are.

Once you've been through this client qualifying process your target short list should now be refined and distilled. It really is a *short* list, because my advice here is to keep things manageable and achievable. For most businesses, or creative agencies, there is no point in having hundreds of companies on your target list. It will become too unwieldy keeping track of them all and the progress will be slower. It's far better to have a properly researched and qualified list of say forty to sixty companies. Perhaps around ten to fifteen per relevant industry sector or category of business. Be rigorous in your short list selection. As I mentioned earlier, they can always change and evolve as you go. This list will become part of your regular reviews – so it's by no means definitive or set in stone.

Now you have your target short list, start thinking about which of your previous or existing clients can be added. This is the time to do a client audit.

The client audit

Whenever I work with a new agency or company, I like to carry out a 'client audit' with them. A client audit is a great way to understand the profile of your business, your existing clients, and your strengths and weaknesses.

What do I mean by a client audit? If you have been in business for a while, simply a detailed look at the profile of the client base of that company going back three to five years. Ask your accounts department (accountants usually like running reports!) to run you a report showing every client of that given time period – a minimum of three and a maximum of five years. If you are a solo creative, look back at your clients from the last few years. You want to see client spend, so you can sort the data to show you where your revenues are coming from. You will be amazed at what kinds of information this throws up. Lapsed clients or people you had forgotten about and projects long since delivered.

If you don't yet have any clients, then use these techniques to start mapping out and visualising your ideal customers. Where are they located? What job roles do they do? What industries are they in?

Lapsed clients are one of the quickest ways for a company to reinvigorate their sales activity. This is a group of clients who liked and trusted you enough to actually spend their money with you. Much of the hard work has already been done with this group of people. You are going to add them to your target short list with the aim of reigniting that relationship. Again, these could be easy wins, and a couple of successes here will boost your confidence.

Arrange a call or send them an email to reconnect in a positive way. (You're not trying to actively 'sell' to them at this stage.). If they're a lapsed client, try to subtly understand what happened. How did they fall by the wayside? Was it you, or was it something on their side? Most companies will happily share this information if you take the trouble to ask. Invariably, if you approach this conversation with the aim of trying to learn something, as opposed to just reconnecting to sell them something, then it will be met far more receptively. Just reconnecting will usually be enough to frame your company in their minds as someone they could work with. It doesn't need to be overtly said in this instance.

There is an option to hold a client survey with your top clients. This is ideally done by a third party so that the client feels they can speak openly, candidly and honestly about your business. A client feedback and brand survey is extremely illuminating. How do clients *really* see your brand? There is often a noticeable disconnect between client and agency; usually around perception and where the strengths and weaknesses are. It's a valuable exercise if you can find the right person to carry it out for you and are willing to embrace the good and not-so-good points about your business!

Referrals

Finally, referrals. Asking for referrals is one of best sources to find clients. You can ask clients (both current and past) as well as people in your network or circle of contacts. There are probably at least two or three new projects in your smartphone that could come via a referral. All you have to do it is ask in the right way. Any request should be timely, credible and polite. If you consider those three things and are humble enough to ask for a bit of help, people are usually very happy to do so. We should all be asking for more referrals in our businesses!

Back to the CRM

In Chapter 5 we looked at establishing a Client Relationship Management system (CRM). This is where you return to that system. Record your target short list. Add your actions and dates of contact. Note any results and set dates for follow-up if appropriate.

Summary

Let's summarise the key parts of the process so far:

Sales plan and strategy
Keep it simple; be stretching but honest and right-sized with your goals. Review regularly.

Brand Proposition
Own a unique space in the market – make it clear and easy to understand. Test it, evaluate it, implement it! Embed it at the heart of your comms and marketing story.

Research and qualifying
Do your homework and understand your clients' businesses. Align them with your proposition. Qualify 'out' rather than qualify 'in'.

Client Audit
Understand what your ideal client profile really looks like. Play to strengths and not your weaknesses.

CRM
Write it all down! Keep it up to date and review it on a regular basis.

Chapter 7

Engaging clients

Now we come to the fun part! The bit where things really start to happen. Or maybe it's the part you fear the most? If so, it really needn't be that way. By now you're beginning to develop an understanding of who you're talking to, what their challenges are and how you can help. Positioning the conversations and prospects like this in your mind will help you to approach this stage with a degree of confidence and help remove some of the fear factor you might be experiencing.

In one of my first ever sales roles I was given a crib sheet to support my telesales calls. I was booking face-to-face appointments for salespeople to go in and try to sell prospective companies a new photocopier. A line on the crib sheet has always stuck in mind: "Remember, if they don't want to talk to you – or worse they are rude – it's not personal and it says more about them than it does about you. It's their loss not yours!"

Again, by reframing the conversation, to recognise the value in what you're doing or offering, is a small but very significant change of focus. The moment you fully believe in what you're doing and are confident in the proposition (and, per earlier, it should be unique) then everything will change. Your whole manner will be more relaxed and confident. Most of this will happen subconsciously and you'll exude a natural confidence that clients will pick up on. It comes from the knowledge about what you're doing and the belief in what you're saying.

Remembering this point is a great anchoring technique in every client conversation, whether on the phone, in an email, during networking or in a meeting:

You are simply trying to grow your company and generate client business.

It is not a bad thing to want to do this – it's the *only thing* that really works when trying to build a business. It's also yet another of the

71

many reasons why Sales needs reframing and a rebrand.

So, if you start to see things through this lens then however ambivalent, or worse rude, a client may be to you then it really won't matter. It is not about you and nor is it personal. It *really is their loss* because it allows you to move on to someone who is receptive and open to conversations about how you can help them and their business. It is a key shift in thinking and perspective, and it works wonders when you're able to get there.

Sales Tip 12: Handling rejection.
Rejections are a fact of life when selling. They will happen, especially at the early stages of conversations, so make your peace with it. It's really not personal. But the flipside of rejection is acceptance. Many clients will engage warmly and respond positively. It's about recognising the two and not getting defeated by the rejections, which most people do.
Don't give up; keep on going but learn and adapt as you go. As an old friend of mine says: "Get to the 'no's and that only leaves the 'yeses'!"

Engaging clients often begins with content that you have generated or written. Perhaps it's some marketing, your website or thought leadership that communicates your vision and ideas. It's important to get your ideas out there and clearly communicate what you do, why you do it and how.

This book is an example of that. I've written it to help you understand how to sell and grow your company more effectively. However, I've also written it to help me grow *my* company more effectively! It's a marketing tool that I hope will generate interest and various sales opportunities. Once you've defined your purpose in the world you can shout about it from the rooftops. I'd like you to try and become 'asset heavy' in your business.

With an abundance of links, blogs, case studies, social posts as tools and hooks that you can fire out there into the world to utilise and engage clients.

The £2-million blog post

I once wrote a blog article for an event production agency I was working with. It was about the challenges of delivering events in Cannes (home of many international business events) and their agency's specific successes in doing so. I took the time to shape and craft the article, and it was a genuinely interesting piece about the various challenges in Cannes when running large-scale events at Cannes Lions and the film festival.

After we'd sent the article out via the agency marketing channels it was viewed by one prospective client more than thirty-five times in just a few days. It turned out they were in the early stages of commissioning a huge bespoke event in Cannes. My agency eventually won the piece of business. In fact, they blew everyone else out the water creatively. By using my effective pitch process, we helped that agency get a deeper understanding of what the client needed. Which gave them a big advantage over the competition. Crucially, we had already positioned them as experts in their space before they even met the client.

That one blog article ultimately led to a £2-million piece of business for the agency.

Yes – you read that correctly. Two-million pounds from one blog post!

The end client admitted that before they had read the article, we weren't even on the pitch list! So, it just goes to show the power of owning a unique idea, clearly communicating it and then getting that marketing content out there to the world. A testament to the power of ideas, original thinking and thought leadership.

Most people focus on the services their company offers, not the true value it delivers. Think about moving your thought process away from the services you offer and instead think about the problems and challenges you help solve. Why did that project work? Why was the client *really* happy? It's usually not so much to do with the services you delivered on a specific project, but on the problem you solved for that client.

By thinking more about the true value (the way you solve a problem) you will unlock the real value in your business or agency.

What is that true value? Articulate it, get it written down and turned into asset. You might have a £2-million blog post on your hands!

Lead generation

Once you've identified who to speak to, and what you're going to say to them, it's now time to start engaging clients. Lead generation will help begin the all-important client conversation. Lead generation is an essential part of building your sales funnel. It's one of the ways to help you drive leads to your business.

There are a whole host of ways you can undertake lead generation. Most of them are effective when managed and implemented in the right way.

These are some of the key ways that agencies and businesses can go about lead generation:

- Broad email marketing
- Telephone/cold calling
- One-2-one email marketing
- LinkedIn connections and emails
- Tech platforms
- Networking
- Referrals
- Social media presence
- Agency/client networking days
- Outsourcing to a third party

All of these have their own strengths and weakness and can be used in different ways. Can you guess which I advocate?

Yes, that's right – all of them.

In various ways I recommend that you try all of these approaches within your business. With the possible exception of agency and client networking days. These are often expensive and run by companies who are motivated by their revenues, not your business development pipeline. However, the rest of these tools are all great ways to start building relationships with clients. You might have mixed feelings about some of them. For instance, telephone-based sales or 'cold calling' fills many people with dread. It's also a controversial topic. Many people argue it's dead, or dying, old-fashioned and no longer has a place in the modern business world.

My own personal view, strictly from a business-to-business (B2B) sales perspective, is this: cold calling is an outdated term that is used by many people to avoid the telephone and talking to people, or clients. Cold calling itself needs a rebrand because it's become a negative and unhelpful term. However, there is still very much a place for a well-researched, well-structured and concise phone call to a client you've not worked with or spoken to before.

Client conversations

Let's do a mini Sales Rebrand right now. Let's rebrand 'cold calls' and instead call them 'client conversations'.

Conversations are what make us human. So, think of this as just talking to people, having a brief informal chat, albeit about business. You have to know what you're going to say, who you're going to talk to, and why they should care. It takes practice and a degree of confidence. Fake it to make it initially. When done right, it is still highly effective. If you want to define that as a cold call, then fine, but the stereotypical image of the cold call is very different to a client conversation.

Phone-based client conversations allow a much more immediate and direct connection with people and clients. A conversation allows you to shine a light on your business, your ideas and ultimately yourself.

Not all clients will be receptive and that's okay. Always be polite, never respond to rudeness by being rude back (not easy but very important) and move on to the next person on your target list. If you've done your homework properly, the people you're calling and the conversations you're having should not feel anything like a cold call. Instead, they're a pleasant, relatively short and engaging conversation.

Here are a few golden rules and tips and pointers when having client conversations on the phone.

- Start with this: "I'm calling you because…" (Be upfront and clear straight away.)
- Lower the tension levels. (Make the person feel at ease.)
- But don't ask how they are – they are fine and will tell you if not. Just get to the point.

- Avoid the um's and er's. (Be bright and bold with your voice.)
- Practise if you can. (Role play before you get started.)
- Keep it short!
- Be yourself.
- Listen for the tone of the other person's voice. (You can tell so much just by their tone.)
- Don't stick to a script but know what you're going to say.
- Build up to the really important calls or clients.
- Warm up before you get to the person you really want to nail a meeting with. (Get into your flow.)
- Recognise yourself and your mood. (Are you happy(ish)?)
- If not do something else.
- Find the time(s) that work best for you. (When do you perform best?)

Don't think of it as a cold call. (It's a client conversation!) There are of course companies who specialise in client conversations for you. There are various lead generation companies who, for a fee, will do the calling part for you. However, some of them are more reputable than others so make sure you do your research before you commission anyone. You will also need to have your own client conversations from time to time. I would therefore urge you to have a go and practise your telephone skills. It's an essential part of selling and will help build your confidence and your business.

These techniques and tips will help you have better conversations with your customers and prospects. They will also lower barriers when talking to any gatekeepers. The more you engage people, the more likely they are to help you.

Key ways to generate leads

Let's look in more detail at some of the key ways to generate leads within your business:

Telephone based Cold calling 'client conversations'

As above, make the time, practise and have a go at picking up the phone from time to time. The phone is your friend, not your enemy.

Email marketing

Great for sharing your ideas to a broader audience and allows you to see who is engaging via the data. However, be careful with data rules such as GDPR (General Data Protection Regulation) and don't over-email. Find a frequency and regularity that is right for your audience. If your unsubscribe rate is high, then you're emailing too often.

One-2-one direct emails

A well-written email can often generate a response. But emails need crafting and shaping with your message. Don't be tempted to just fire them off without asking: 'Why should the recipient care?' Emails are also very easy to delete and very ignorable. In isolation they will not grow your business. They are part of the mix, not a complete strategy.

LinkedIn connections and emails

LinkedIn is a great tool for researching and finding out who your clients and prospects are. Try personalising a message when you invite them to link in with you. Don't get too excited when they accept (many people automatically do) and think about how you can engage or interest them further. Leave it a short while before asking for a call or meeting.

Networking

Networking is a great way to meet clients and it takes many forms, either face to face at relevant business events or online via video conferencing. A quick google in your sector or industry will throw up many events that are a good fit for your business. When at an event, the same rules as the telephone apply; don't bore people! Keep it short, concise and ask them about themselves more than you talk about yourself. Set a target of a minimum number of events per month or quarter. One a week is good to start with.

Events

Organising and hosting your own events is a great way to get a group of clients in a room and showcase your ideas. These can be regular, ad hoc or informal. Breakfast briefings are always popular as clients can then start their day after the event. Choose a good venue and make it enticing. You don't need to oversell; think more about how you can make the event valuable and dynamic, so you send them away happy. You can follow up afterwards and you are now on their radar.

Referrals

This is something most people don't do enough. When a project has gone well it's a great thing to ask: "Do you know anyone else who might benefit from our services?" Most happy clients are usually willing to help. Referrals usually lead to a conversion and sale in one form or another simply because the person referring has already done much of the qualifying. Make it a rule to ask for more referrals from your clients and wider network.

Social

As with email marketing, social media is not an entire sales or lead generation strategy in isolation. It's a brilliant tool for building your brand and market visibility, but on its own it won't be enough. You have to incorporate it within your other activities. Make sure your content is unique and engaging whilst also being aligned to your USPs and brand proposition. Content, and the way you use it on social media, can be very powerful – as I outlined earlier with the £2-million blog post.

Agency/client networking days

This is a relatively new area of lead generation that has sprung up in the last few years. The organisers invite a group of clients to a day of meetings, on the premise that they will get to meet some exciting new agencies. Those agencies pay handsomely to be in the room. It can be effective, and plenty of people win business. But it's also expensive and can be a bit of a lottery as to the client rapport and overall interest. I would approach these events with caution.

Outsourcing

If you don't feel like doing any of these things, then you can always outsource! There are plenty of companies and people who can help in all of these areas. However, by doing so, ask yourself if it is taking you away from the sharp end of business development. You will still need to be involved in the sales efforts for your company. Delegating responsibility is not an effective strategy. These outsourcing companies are best utilised when you work closely with them rather than removing yourself from the process. Keep your contracts and trial periods short so that you can get out of them if people don't deliver.

Meetings

All your lead generation has worked, and you now have a diary chock full of meetings with new prospective clients. Congratulations! This is a great start, and you are now halfway there. How should you approach these meetings? What's the best way to structure them? How can you ensure the right outcome for you and for the client?

You might be someone that loves meeting people and are entirely comfortable in face-to-face situations. Many people are. However, you *might* be someone that doesn't enjoy meetings, especially with clients you've never met before.

Understanding where your own levels of acceptance, and performance, is at with face-to-face meetings is important. If you're a star that likes to shine, then great, embrace it. The floor is yours and you have the stage – do what you do best. As long as you involve and engage the other parties present in the appropriate ways, i.e. – don't make it all about you! Boring someone or talking nonstop for twenty minutes is the worst thing you can do.

Meetings are fundamentally about building trust and rapport. You do that initially by being polite, curious, professional and having complete integrity to your approach. Questions first, your own views and statements second. As I've said earlier, do your homework on the client and their business so that, to a degree, you can see things from their perspective. Most of all you should be asking questions.

Questions that are designed to get the other person talking. Talking more than you do! Open questions allow you to build information and start to develop the client relationship.

If you're less of a talker, and perhaps a bit more reserved in meetings, think about ways that you can work around that. Asking more questions than talking, for example. Having a pre-planned framework or structure on what you're going to say will also help. Perhaps taking someone with you who can support you and create a tag team effect.

I've worked with many, many different people and leaders in creative businesses. There are those that like to 'shoot from the hip' and who take a very relaxed style to any meeting. Then there are those who like to plan everything down to the last detail; they always have a pre-prepared agenda and know exactly what they want to say. Human beings are of course highly unpredictable creatures! You do often get a clash of styles. Introvert meets extrovert is always an interesting one to observe.

Flexibility and adaptability are highly important. It's essential to be prepared and ready to go off-piste, to work with the person you're meeting, and not against them to your own agenda. It sounds obvious but so many people overlook this simple rule. They often give up, or worse lose interest, when the client throws in a curve ball. The more you're ready for the curve ball to happen (and it will happen a lot) the more successful you will be. Sometimes clients like to be mischievous or ask the difficult questions you hadn't thought of. Be ready for them and not thrown by them.

One of my past clients was best described as a human hand grenade. Largely a charming person, he was good company and clients liked meeting him. However, he had an unfortunate tendency to say something deliberately awkward or controversial at exactly the wrong moment. I think he did it mostly to get a reaction. It was excruciating and you never knew when he would go off and explode. I'm sure it lost him lots of business over the years!

Another meeting with a Middle Eastern client took me four years to secure. Four years of me asking to meet, booking the time, and then it being cancelled a few days prior. I eventually sat down with him for tea at a London hotel to discuss a pitch. The first thing he said was:

"Apologies, Rob, we've been trying to meet for a little while". I didn't remind him it was four years! He did then give me a film production worth £1.5 million, so it was worth the wait.

It's also okay to say you don't know the answer sometimes. Don't make something up – they'll spot it a mile off and you'll end up in a dead end with no rapport or relationship. Just be upfront and honest if you don't know. You'll be respected more when you do.

The more meetings you do the better you'll get at them. As with any sales activity it's all about regularity and practice. Some meetings will go fantastically well and leave both you and the client feeling energised and inspired – like you've conquered the world. Others will leave you feeling flat and demotivated.

Client meetings vary, so look out for, and try to spot, any patterns. What went well, what didn't? When and where are your most effective meetings taking place? Learn from them all the time so that you can adapt and make changes as you go. Ask clients for feedback too; they'll appreciate your openness and you'll get invaluable honest feedback from them.

There are lots of ways to approach your meetings with clients. The key is to know your own style and work with it.

Own your strengths and play to them!

Meeting rules, signals and suggestions

Here are some of the golden rules to follow when it comes to client meetings. You can use this as a checklist that you refer back to, before and after meetings. Although, it goes without saying –never during meetings. Clients should always, always have your full attention! Eventually this list will become second nature and will help you read pretty much any situation, client reactions and form a view on their overall levels of interest. If things are *not* going as expected, you can use these signals and rules to do something about it and take action to change the course of a meeting and conversation.

Be prepared
Rule number 1. Don't rock up having not done your homework. At the very least a quick look at their website, or LinkedIn profile. Make the

person feel like you care enough to have put some time in. If you really haven't had the time, try to at least give the impression that you have, but don't bullshit – you'll get found out!

Questions

You should be asking a lot of questions. Use words and phrases like 'What...?' 'How...?' or 'Tell me...' in front of any question you ask. This open question technique will help get the target client talking and opening up because it prompts them to talk. Avoid closed questions that invite just 'yes'/'no' answers. 'Why?' can be quite defensive, too, so use sparingly.

Time

Think about the best time to set the meeting. When would suit the client? When would suit you? Do you perform best in the morning or at the end of the day? Personally, I never meet anyone on a Friday afternoon. It feels like people are winding down and have subconsciously 'clocked off'. I don't want to be largely forgotten about come the following week. Similarly, Mondays are a busy 'doing' day for most people, so I rarely have face-to-face meetings on a Monday. Therefore, that leaves me a window of three days.

Block book

This is a great way to get into a rhythm with your meetings. Try block booking your schedule with around two to five meetings per day. You will be more in your flow with client conversations and more dynamic. It's also a far more effective use of your diary and frees up the other days for clear productivity. I use block booking a lot, particularly on international trips, and it works extremely well.

One simple idea

Aim to leave the client with a simple idea. Most people forget 80% of what is said in a meeting. Therefore, start and finish the meeting on one simple easy-to-remember idea or concept. Ideally, this one simple idea should be aligned to your brand, story or unique proposition. You can use it as an opening or closing statement and it's highly memorable, especially when told as a story.

Slides

A few slides or examples are okay but obviously avoid 'death by PowerPoint'. You should be talking and conversing rather than presenting. The more detailed product information can come later. Early meetings are about building rapport. You don't do that with slides.

Don't bore them

See above. Don't bore them or talk at them. (NB: You might not be aware you're doing this, so ask peers for honest feedback as you refine your meeting technique.)

Frame the agenda

Be clear about the aims of the meeting. Have you understood the client's agenda, and are you both aligned? Be clear on timings and what you're going to cover. Ask the client for their input!

Make it human

Once you've got the business stuff out of the way, and there is good chemistry or rapport between you, allow the human side to come through. Be yourself and explore the personalities. Asking some golden nugget-type questions will help you learn more about them as people.

Golden nuggets

When deployed correctly, asking golden nugget-type questions is a great way of understanding what makes other people tick. Typical gold nuggets might be:

- Where do they live?
- What are their interests, hobbies or passions?
- Do they have family?

I suggest you only ask once you have good rapport with someone. This will probably be at the end of the meeting. However, don't overdo it, as it's a fine line between friendly interest and vacuousness. Get the balance right. After the meeting, write down those personal nuggets and remember them for the next meeting. The client will be impressed that you've remembered, and the fact that you've bothered shows you are genuinely interested in them.

Be present
Our friend the phone again. Ideally your phone (and laptop) should not even be in the room with you. Be 100% present with the client and give them your full, undivided attention. There's always a temptation to check messages (WhatsApp has a lot to answer for) but don't do it! Give them your time and attention, and the person will feel truly valued.

Agree next steps
Always agree some clear next steps and actions by the end of the meeting. Ensure you always stick to yours, even if they don't. Make sure you send anything you promised in a timely manner. If you can, get the second meeting pencilled in the diary whilst you're both there in person.

Things to watch out for

Your performance
How are you feeling? Are you prepared and relaxed? If not, what can you do to get yourself into a prepared and relaxed state? Clearing the diary for some prep time? Going for a walk? Some breathing exercises? Make a cup of tea or coffee? What is the best way for you to take a five-minute break and reset before any important meeting?

Their performance
How is the client behaving? Do they seem relaxed and happy to talk? Or do they seem bored and disinterested? Don't be thrown by it if they do – ask them what they'd like to get out of the time.

Body language
Watching out for body language signals and facial expressions will help you read a person's mood and engagement. How are they sitting – are they slumped back or leaning towards you? Leaning in is a good 'interested' signal, whereas the reverse is also probably true. Are people frowning as they listen to you? They could be finding you hard to understand. If they're smiling and their arms are unfolded that would

suggest openness and a relaxed engaged manner. Learning to read body language is a great habit to get into. Watch and observe people and you'll soon pick up useful cues.

The reliable muscles

These are the facial muscle that people cannot help moving. They happen automatically in direct response to whatever is going on for them! The reliable muscles include the eyes, eyebrows, forehead, mouth and cheeks. You can literally read what a person is experiencing by the way their face moves. Best of all they are doing it completely automatically (unless they're a very sophisticated poker player) as it's part of our DNA and inherent human nature. Practise looking at and reading the reliable muscles because they will tell you a lot. A good tip is to watch TV news and watch the facial reactions and responses of two people in a live interview discussion.

Tension levels

Part of your job in any meeting is to help lower the natural and instinctive tension levels that will be present. As human beings, tension is hardwired into us because it helps us to approach any new or unfamiliar situations with a degree of wariness. Once you know this, you can work with it and not let the nerves (theirs and yours) get in the way. Create an environment to allow this to happen and make people feel at ease. Ask questions that help build rapport and trust. Offer a suggested agenda, be clear with your aims – and always ask them about theirs. Get those tension levels down as quickly as you can.

Talking too much

Get the balance right and don't talk more than the client – unless they expressly ask you to do so.

Networking events

Life is a pitch. Never a truer word said, particularly with creative businesses. We are constantly pitching in the creative industry, and pitching is truly an art form in itself. We usually need to pitch at networking events, and these can take many forms – from large conferences of several hundred people to breakfast or drinks sessions with just a handful.

A few years ago, I met a lady called Anna at a networking event. Anna worked for a global law firm, and we had a conversation of no more than a few minutes about our businesses and backgrounds. It was polite, had an element of small talk, but was business-like and friendly.

A few weeks afterwards, I went to Anna's office and had a meeting with her and the marketing team within the law firm. It was a very tentative early-stage conversation for us both. In truth, I suspect neither of us thought there was a huge amount of business we would do together. However, we got on well. There was good natural rapport and so the meeting was certainly worth our time.

Around two years later, I had an email from Anna out of the blue. She had a client in town looking for an agency – would I like to meet him? Obviously, I didn't have to think about it too long before saying 'yes'. Anna's client turned out to be an international energy company. Quite literally, one of the world's biggest companies that very few people have ever heard of. (Remember this from Chapter 6: it pays to find the hidden gems – those under-the-radar clients that nobody else is looking for.)

To date, my agency client has now delivered work with this company and the total billing currently is £1.7 million and counting. That figure all came as a direct result of meeting Anna, having a quick chat at a networking event, and bothering to follow it up. It's not an uncommon occurrence to win business like this when you take the time to get out there and network. There are thousands and thousands of other Annas in the world waiting to connect you to their clients. But you must be able to communicate what you do, and your value, clearly – otherwise *your* Anna won't introduce you!

Sales tip 13: Network more.
Find your Annas in the world. They are out there if you turn those antennae on and start recognising the connectors you meet or who are already in your world. We're now more connected than ever before. This presents an opportunity if you use it in the right way.

The elevator pitch

There are plenty of things you can do to make networking events more effective for you, and one of these is to prepare and polish your 'elevator pitch'. I've attended hundreds of networking events and I've always been surprised at the varying degrees of success with social or classic 'elevator' pitches.

So, what is the elevator pitch? It's you introducing yourself and what you do in a succinct and interesting way. You probably have thirty seconds to make a good impression with your elevator pitch, so it's definitely something you should work on and refine before you find yourself on the spot. The elevator pitch is a golden opportunity to make a great first impression.

The moment to use your elevator pitch comes when you hear questions like: "What do you do?" or... "What kind of business are you in?"

I've heard some fairly confusing answers to that question recently. Some of them, in fact, have been downright terrible. Along the lines of...

"So, what do you do?"

"I run a B2B/B2C, geo locator app plug-in that increases proximity marketing for geo tagging and meta data tracking for large scale consumer brands and IP rights holders."

Horrendous. My mind glazed over instantly. That was an actual pitch that someone said to me, I kid you not.

Instead, keep it simple and human, and focus on the benefit you deliver. The aim is to leave the person you're talking to excited and ready to talk, not totally baffled and ready to move away from you.

Try saying something like this instead...

"I've built an app that helps big brands understand where their customers are and what they're doing in different locations. Our technology gives brands information that increases their sales conversions and ultimately helps grow my clients' businesses."

A great elevator pitch should leave the person who hears it feeling enlightened, engaged and intrigued to find out more about you and your business. (The opposite emotional responses are confused, bored and disengaged but most people are way too polite to ever tell you that's how they're feeling!)

Here are some suggestions on how to make a great elevator pitch in a social or business networking environment:

- **Start with 'why'** – tell the person why you do what you do. Why does your business exist? What gets you out of bed in the morning? Why are you passionate about it? What gets you excited?
- **Have confidence** – be bold and be self-assured. This is your chance to shine and make an impact so don't blow it by mumbling, looking at the floor (or far worse, over the person's shoulder) and speaking incoherently. If you struggle with these things, practise and try it out on friends and colleagues until your confidence improves.
- **Tell a story** – try and put some emotive storytelling into your elevator pitch. We all love a good story, so think about your own personal experiences. Cold hard logic and facts about why your business is brilliant are not enough on their own. Remember: logic makes people think; emotion makes people act.
- **Be passionate** – delivering your elevator pitch should get you excited. Your face should light up when asked what you do. If you aren't excited by it, then why should the person you are talking to be?
- **Jargon buster** – avoid jargon. I'll say that again: avoid jargon! There is already too much of it in business today. If you really want to speak technically and dazzle them with your business brilliance, then fine – but keep it for later. The time for showing technical brilliance isn't during your elevator pitch. That can come later, when you have more time with a potential client, and they already have a sense of what you do and how you can help them.
- **Keep it simple** – as human beings we usually like to get things straight away, so keep it very, very simple, at least initially. Don't make it any harder than it needs to be for the person you're talking with to understand what you do. A good test is, would your granny or a ten-year-old child understand what you do if you told them? That might sound too simplistic but trust

me, that's a better place to start than confusing the hell out of someone and then trying to clarify it.

- **Add value** – you've covered why you do what you do. Now think value. What's in it for your clients? How do you deliver value and help them or their business? Think value, impact and results. Which aspects of your elevator pitch will they relate to – and where's the value for them?

- **Practice makes perfect** – rehearse, rehearse and rehearse again. Change your elevator pitch – multiple times if needed. There is, of course, no such thing as perfection but there is certainly no harm in trying!

- **Enjoy it** – pitching is a great way to share experiences, tell people about your business and get feedback on what you're doing. Keep an open mind and most of all, have fun and enjoy it. It's all part of the big game we play called business. The more you enjoy and practise any game, usually the more you enjoy it.

- **Learn and improve** – once you've done all of these things, practised your new communication skills and begun to make consistently good pitches, understand what's working and what isn't. Are there specific aspects of your business you need to focus more or less on? Have you noticed people respond better to certain phrases you're using? Now it's time to observe, listen and improve.

Use your team to share and discuss ideas. Get a sales buddy or put a team in place for new business.

> **Sales Tip 14: Spread the load.**
> Engaging clients is much easier when there is more than one of you.
> A second or third pair of eyes will get you there much quicker.

If you're a solo entrepreneur, joining a business networking group or getting a mentor is a great way to do this. Someone to help share the challenges and provide some support as you go, through the difficult moments and help remind you any rejection is not personal. They will also help you enjoy and recognise the successes more, too.

Summary

Marketing and thought leadership

Get your ideas out there to the world. Make them interesting, unique and relevant so that clients see your value and how you can help them. People want to see your best thinking and ideas. Don't be afraid to put them out there.

Lead generation

Take a holistic 360-degree approach and try different things for your business. Keep it consistent and regular. Don't give up when you hit setbacks! Consider outsourcing if it helps but keep the contracts short and make them very target-orientated.

Meetings

Don't waste the golden opportunity of a client meeting. They are very hard to get. Make sure you're prepared, researched and ready. Know your style and play to it.

Networking

An essential part of sales and business development. You never know when the next client, project or deal is coming from. Don't bore people or confuse them when networking. Keep it simple!

Elevator pitch

Refine your elevator pitch and practise it so you can deliver smoothly when prompted.

Chapter 8

Winning clients

Winning clients is the stage when everything finally starts to come together. If you combine just some of the elements and suggestions in previous chapters, then things will start to happen. Winning clients is the fun bit – and of course it's the essential part. Winning a new client, or several, has the potential to transform and revolutionise your business. In some ways it's also one of the most delicate and challenging parts of the Sales process.

By this stage in the game, you should have so much information and knowledge about a client or specific situation. But how best to use it? Knowledge is power, after all. Where should you pitch yourselves or your ideas? Does price or budget play a major factor?

Invariably, yes. So, ask yourself some more questions:

- What process is the client following?
- Will there be a lengthy pitch process?
- How do you negotiate with the client?

The pitch process

Let's start with the pitch process and recap some of my previous points.

Anyone who tells you that you can win without pitching is, for the most part, talking nonsense. Any major client or project these days will involve *some kind of* pitch. Even if the client is single sourcing (directly choosing just one supplier to provide for them) then you will probably still have to pitch your vision or ideas in response to their brief. Therefore, it's worth taking them through an effective pitch or buying process so that you can be confident you've responded in the very best way possible.

On the subject of single sourcing, invariably there will be more

91

than one person or agency joining the party. I say this from years of frontline sales activity with numerous agencies. Experience tells me it's very rare that a big client will just award a major piece of business without doing their due diligence and, at the very least, getting other quotes or competitive bids. I wish it wasn't always so, but it usually is. Furthermore, anti-bribery and competition laws are continually being looked at and monitored in most countries. This is a good thing and gone are the days of the backhander or dodgy dealings that don't allow a level, fair playing field.

'A pitch', then, can mean many things. It can mean a competitive bid situation in the classic sense of the word. It can also mean a one-to-one buying conversation with a client. It could just be a chat in a coffee shop. Pitching is a broad term that will mean many things to your business.

An effective pitch process is therefore highly important. It's the final hurdle that you must overcome. Accordingly, a great pitch process is a big weapon that you can deploy in your arsenal. It will help you overcome the competition.

I've been through many, many pitch processes in my life. Some of them are just one-to-one credentials-style conversations. Others – the good ones – are for major pieces of businesses. (By the way, it feels amazing when you win one of these and absolutely devastating when you lose one!)

But here's the thing….I don't fear pitches. Generally, I welcome them. Why? Because I know I can go through a pitch process better than most people. I know that the tools I've got, and that the questions I'll ask, will allow me to understand what the client's objectives really are, usually far better than my competitors. This process allows me, and my agency clients, to really get under the skin of what people are looking for. It helps me dig deeper, find out more and usually win my pitch.

This has been learnt through hard work and lots of experience, however. It wasn't always the case that I was so willing to embrace any big pitch. There are both good and bad examples, and all of them have helped shape my process and method to date.

Probably one of my worst pitches ever happened a few years ago…

It was with a global insurance company in the City of London.

The pitch time was arranged for 9am on a Monday morning. In hindsight, we should never have agreed to that. There was no leeway if things went wrong, which in this case they did. I had the pitch deck on my laptop and stupidly it was not backed up on a memory stick or online. As I arrived at the offices, in good time for the meeting, I turned on my laptop. Windows immediately started to run a mandatory software update. Quoted finishing time ninety minutes!

I cannot tell you the horror I felt at that moment as the laptop slowly started to crawl through the update, stuck on 9% for a good twenty minutes. My agency client then arrived and the two of us had no alternative but to go into the meeting. We made our excuses and offered our profuse apologies. There was no other option but to describe the idea, without any kind of visual or presentation to show them.

In short, it was a disaster. A total car crash. The main insurance client sat there and glowered at me throughout whilst her senior colleagues did their best to be polite about the situation. I can smile about this now because, a few months later, I helped the agency win their biggest ever project. But it was a very valuable lesson in being prepared for things to go disastrously wrong. Always, always have a backup.

Structuring an effective pitch

What is the best way of structuring an effective pitch? How can you take a client through a process that will greatly increase your chances of success?

The key is to start building knowledge and information about the project straight away. You can do this by asking pertinent questions that reveal the client's underlying aims and objectives about the project. In doing this, you will start to frame your business or agency in the mind of the client. They will start to think: "Hmm, these guys are asking all of the right questions – their thinking is good".

Structuring an effective pitch is all about positioning and digging deeper. With a bit of luck, other companies pitching *will not* be asking these kinds of questions. Or certainly they won't be asking them as efficiently – which will make *you* stand out even more! By the time you walk into the room to deliver your pitch, your aim is to have understood what they are looking for so well, that your creative idea or presentation is something of a formality. It will be so aligned with the client's goals that they will instantly want to say, "Yes – you're hired". When managed in the right way, this is a process that works time and time again.

Structuring an effective pitch is the single biggest tool that has helped me win more revenues than anything else in my business. So, it's a good one to learn and implement in your business asap.

Let's look at the buying funnel to work through the process:

Buying Model

- What / How / Tell me...
- What is your vision for this project?
- What does success look like?

1 Respond / question / listen

- If we did X,Y,Z how would that feel?
- What are your budget parameters?
- What challenges or barriers are there to overcome?

2 Challenge / interrogate

- Idea development and design iterations
- Creative Solutions - value delivery
- What is the client selection criteria - are you aligned?

3 Interpret / create

- Evaluate your creative and technical ideas
- Is your solution right?
- Test... challenge... qualify...

4 Question

- Put yourself in the client shoes
- Have you fulfilled the brief?
- Question & understand - more client discussion?

5 Evaluate

6 Deliver

- Rehearse, Rehearse Rehearse!
- Know who will be in the room
- Where do we go from here?

GO!

Starting at the top, let's work through each part of the funnel:

Listen/question/respond

This is arguably the most important phase of any pitch conversation. Take the time to listen and learn. Ask to speak to the client once they've invited you to pitch – either in person (if they will agree to it) or via a phone call. Often neither of these will be permitted, in which case ask to send through a list of questions. If the client still refuses to answer any questions, be very wary. Is this something you realistically have a chance of winning? Most likely not and you could just be making up the numbers. You can always decline. Remember you don't have to say 'yes'! However, if they do agree to talk, remember the open question technique to get them talking and opening up. Respond with relevant appropriate thoughts as you go, to test their thinking and reactions. Ask bold, strong questions such as: "What does success look like for you?" or, "What do we need to do to win the business?" These are great ways to learn what the client is thinking.

Challenge and interrogate

There is a place for appropriately challenging and testing some thoughts or ideas. As long as you have good rapport with the client, you can ask relatively direct questions. This is the time to go a bit deeper: "If we suggested X,Y,Z, how would that feel?" Another great question to ask is: "On a scale of one to ten where do you want to be creatively? One being very safe and conservative, and ten being off the scale creatively." You will get very different responses to this question! The client's answers and reactions will help shape your creative thinking at a later stage, so make sure you take the time to do this.

Interpret/create

Once you've understood the client's thinking, you can now go away and begin your creative thinking. This is your time to start interpreting the client's objectives and translating them into your ideas. Do what you do best – that's why they're interested in you and that's why you're on the pitch list!

Question

By now you should be confident in what the client is looking for and confident in your ability to win the pitch. If you're not confident at this stage, ask yourself whether it is time to bow out. Would your time be better spent elsewhere?

Once a plan is beginning to formulate in your mind, consider whether you can go back to the client and test the water. By checking your thinking with them, you can sense-check if they like it. It's also a great way of keeping the dialogue going. Inevitably you will pick up more information and more nuggets the more you talk to the client. If they're happy to keep chatting (which often they are) – do it! However, make sure you don't give away the big reveal until you need to. Keep most of the big creative input back for now. All you're looking to do at this stage is check that you are on the right track and your thinking is aligned with their success factors.

Evaluate

Ask yourself as you go: "Are we fulfilling the brief here?" Your job as the salesperson is to become the eyes and ears of the client, especially if you're working in a team and other creatives are having an input into the overall pitch. Sometimes creatives will get fixated on a particular idea that *you* know is not right. If this happens, it's your job (often my job) to challenge back internally. It isn't always an easy conversation to have but, trust me, it's much better than losing the pitch because the idea wasn't right and you didn't say anything to the other members of your team. Always try to think like the client and use their success factor and objectives. Evaluate as you go, and don't be afraid to change course if you need to.

Deliver

You've come up with a brilliant creative idea or proposal. Now you have to go and deliver it. The thing to do at this point is to decide who is going to be in the room. Think about the personalities involved and avoid any clashes. You want your best self, or your A-team delivering their A-game. So, choose a time that best suits you. Try to avoid the middle slot if clients are block booking. Going either first or last is usually a better bet for making an impact. This is surprisingly effective at helping win more pitches – especially if you know you've nailed the creative. Get in there early, dazzle them and leave everyone else looking average. It works!

You should also know who will be in the room from their side and what their individual agenda is. Are they focussed on the budget or the creative? Do they want the detail or the sizzle? You should know this because you've asked the question. Don't be thrown if the Chairman or MD has turned up for the pitch (it happens) because you didn't bother to find out who is coming. Lastly, rehearse, rehearse, rehearse! Practise so that your performance is polished and impressive. Be ready for the difficult, challenging questions – embrace them head on, and don't fear them.

GO!

By doing all of this and following the process you will have now built a dialogue with the client throughout the pre-pitch period. By the time you walk into that room to deliver the pitch, or send it digitally via email, you will be so aligned with the client that you are making it very easy for them to say 'yes'. You have framed your company, your team and you as the only people that they should be awarding this project to. It is the natural choice for them to say 'yes' and press the big green GO button! You have made it easy for them to buy from you. This is ultimately what selling is all about.

Pricing your services

Knowing how to price your products and services is both an art and a science. In fact, it's often a blend of art versus science in order to get the right balance. Obviously, there is no definitive rule other than to be competitive and affordable. At a level where the client is able to buy and you're able to make a decent and sustainable profit. If you are neither, then you'll price yourself out of the market.

Know the broad market value for your services. If you don't have this information then perhaps consider carrying out some research. Find out what your competitors are charging or what clients see as the true value for a range of goods and services. Carry out a survey or ask people for a few short calls. The information you gather will help you build your own pricing structure.

Don't be tempted to undercut and slash your costs in order to win every job. From time to time, you might want to do this, perhaps to win a particular client. However, it shouldn't be a regular occurrence, or you will soon go out of business. Remember, one of the main reasons you are in business is to make a profit. If you're not able to make a profit (after covering *all* of your overhead costs) then you don't have a viable business model. This is a really important point that many businesses fail to grasp, especially creative businesses. It's your duty as the business owner (or key salesperson) to understand the basic concept of profit, loss and gross margin on the projects you are selling. If you don't understand the financials, then ask somebody financially literate to help you. For a few hundred pounds or dollars a year an accountant can help guide you through. (They will also keep you out of trouble with the taxman.) This is money very well spent!

Many businesses, particularly start-ups, tend to price themselves too cheaply in the hope of winning the client. This is a mistake as it creates a mismatch between your true worth and what you are delivering for the client. Plus, you will eventually start to resent your client. There is often a hope that, by securing their business for a lower price, you can win the client and impress them enough to make up higher fees later on. This rarely works.

Another temptation is to work with a start-up client, who themselves have very low budgets. The theory is that as the client grows, they will take the creative agency with them. Be careful about doing this as it rarely works out that way. As client companies grow, so too do their ambitions. What tends to happen is people quietly forget the little guys who helped them in the early stages. Often grandiose ideas (and usually a bit of ego) kicks in and they start hiring big expensive creative agencies. I've seen it happen all too often. Choose your clients wisely, especially start-ups.

As you develop your business you will learn more and more about your prices and where you fit in to the market. It's a constant exercise in listening, learning and understanding the information coming from the market and your clients.

In other words – it's a Sales exercise!

Pricing Rules

- Don't be too cheap – think premium as much as possible.
- Don't be too prohibitively expensive either – ultimately your clients need to be able to afford you.
- Know the market rates and where you fit in.
- What is your pricing strategy – are you a budget or premium offering?
- Being known for being premium, or expensive, is okay as long as you demonstrate why and actually sell something to your clients. It's no good being premium and never making any revenues!

- Believe in your prices and have conviction with your approach – bold confidence.
- Let your fees reflect the true value of you and your business.
- Always, always, ask the client what their budget is.
- If they categorically won't tell you, sound them out with some options. For example "If I said we charged $10,000 for a similar project recently, how would that feel?" Their reaction and answer will tell you a lot. (You can vary the amount to suit your business $10K, $50K, $1M etc.)
- Your business needs a specific and bespoke pricing structure.

Negotiation

Negotiation is an art form in itself and it's a skill you will eventually need to learn and practise within your business. During the latter stages of a client conversation, you will need to have a basic understanding of negotiation principles in order to get the best possible outcomes for you and your company.

There are many forms of negotiation, but your focus should be on commercial negotiation. We are not focussed here on political negotiation or any other kind. Purely commercial negotiation.

Commercial negotiation can be defined as 'the exchange of value between two parties'. So, where should you start?

You must know whereabouts on a sliding scale you are negotiating. At one end you have cold, hard negotiations. These are purely price led and it's all about bartering or haggling for the best possible prices. At the other end of the scale, you have the warmer side of negotiations, which involve more trust and have more elements than just purely price, although it's still a factor.

Understanding where your negotiation is taking place is the first stage. Is the client (or their procurement team) just trying to beat you down on price? Negotiating with procurement teams is an art you must master in creative businesses. It's their job to get the best price and terms for their organisation. It's your job not to give in or accept without negotiating the best outcome for *your* business.

There are several ways that you can improve your chances of success, for instance, setting a price that has a degree of 'wiggle room' built into it. You can do this more aggressively at the cold end of the negotiation scale.

Let's take a classic example of bartering, say in a Moroccan souk where a trader is selling a beautiful traditional clay tagine. The trader sees his well-heeled tourist with her expensive sunglasses, latest iPhone in hand and $1200 designer sneakers on her feet. She enters his shop and is clearly interested in buying the tagine; it would make a lovely gift for her parents at home. "Hello" he thinks, cartoon dollar signs whizzing through his eyes.

Negotiations open. The trader tries his luck at five times the market rate and says the price is $120. The tourist, herself no fool, knows this so she counters with a very low-ball offer at $25. They have now both done what's known as 'opening extreme'. They have set a price with a very large margin for manoeuvre on the extreme end for each of them. This is also known as the bargaining range – or the gap between those two opening prices. It's a technique that you can use on any cooler price-led negotiation. Knowing where to 'open' is something you must instinctively gauge, and you can usually be more bullish (or extreme) than you think.

The trader soon realises his mark is no pushover. Thus, a lively and rapid haggle begins with each countering the other. The tourist appears to really want to buy the tagine. However, the trader hasn't made any sales for the last four hours and the cash would be a welcome boost to his day. Each of them has their own pressure points and demands that are motivating their bids. They are currently haggling between the two prices that each of them opened on.

The sliding scale between the two prices is the bargaining range. The buyer needs to secure the purchase for as near to their opening price as they can. For the vendor the reverse is true – he is trying to get the buyer as close as possible to his opening price. Therefore, you want to 'open extreme' and know where in the 'bargaining range' your own cut-off point is.

Remember that most, if not all, negotiations at this cooler end of the scale are low trust in terms of the broader long-term relationship. Think about when you sell your house or your car... you're very unlikely to ever see the new owners of your house again. All you want is the best possible price for what is probably the biggest asset you own.

It's the same when you are buying – all you're generally concerned with is achieving the best possible deal for you. Opening extreme is a technique you can use on many things – not just a tagine!

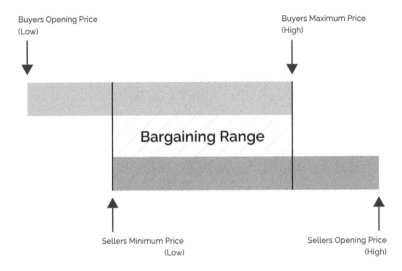

In the end the tourist agrees to buy the tagine for $45. The trader is happy with this, and it represents a good price for his first sale of the day. However, they both walk away wondering what better price they *could* have got. You should too. You should never walk away thinking that what you agreed was a great deal. *Always* consider what better price they might have accepted. Try it next time you're in a market or shop and notice the dynamics of bartering or haggling. It just takes a bit of practice.

On bigger projects the warmer your negotiations, the more trust there will be involved. Price will still be a factor but there are likely to be a variety of other elements to the negotiation. Things like payment and contractual terms, delivery milestones, quantities and shipping costs. Perhaps you might also be negotiating on marketing budgets or clearance rights for a specific project. Everything must be considered from the outset before you go into the negotiation. The other party is not just looking for a price-led haggle. They are looking for trust and reciprocity, and this can mean the negotiation will be more complex. These are important values for you to consider as you prepare. Try to avoid the competitive ego creeping in because you have to seek a way to help cede satisfaction to the other party. This is essential to understanding where the balance of power lies and working out how you can help the other party achieve their goals whilst simultaneously achieving yours.

The key to doing all of this is preparation. Eighty per cent of any commercial negotiation is in the preparation – even before you meet the other party and get down to business.

Let's look at some of the key points to consider when negotiating:

- Understand where on the scale your negotiations are taking place – warm or cold / bartering or haggling. Or trust and high value.
- Prepare as much as possible – understand the other party's perspective and then use it to your advantage.
- Plan your moves in advance.
- Exercise control and discipline – don't let emotion get in the way.
- Look out for buying signals – what information is the other party giving away?
- Negotiating is uncomfortable at times – especially in the final moments. When people are trying to influence you. *Know this and understand it.* Get comfortable with the discomfort and learn to live with it. Recognise it when it's happening. People say 'yes' to make themselves feel better and more comfortable.
- Try saying 'no' when you feel like saying 'yes' – try it a few times on smaller conversations.
- When you say 'yes' it devalues your 'no'.
- Don't end up negotiating for the sake of it – or for the sake of principle. Better to see the bigger picture and cede satisfaction to the other party in order to get your outcomes.
- Understand *perceived* value versus *real* value.

Winning work

You've done it! Congratulations!

You have nailed the client pitch process and the important client conversations. The relationship is in a very strong place and, above all, the client has selected you as their preferred partner. That is no mean feat, so well done. It's truly a great feeling – enjoy it.

However, keep in mind that you should not break out the champagne straight away. Always be cautious, even at these final stages. A deal is not won or in the bag until you have a signed contract or an official purchase order. It can be tempting to celebrate and start hiring or spending for the project straight away. Don't do it! A lot of things can still change or go wrong, even in these final stages.

Be very clear in what you're asking the client to do in order to proceed. Will you use your contract or theirs? What's the agreed time frame? Make sure you are very clear and confident in what your process is so that both of you know the timeline and key project milestones.

During the project a salesperson's job is to be the eyes and ears of the client in the background – is the project on track? Is the client happy? Are you noticing signals or things that indicate otherwise? Have the account team or project delivery folks missed any of them? It's your job as the person who has built the relationship, and ultimately sold the project, to keep an eye on the key success factors.

You probably won't be closely involved in detailed delivery but think of yourself as the internal client representative. Don't be afraid to speak up and challenge your colleagues from time to time. Again, these are not always easy conversations to have. However, it is better that you have them pre-emptively so that the client does not come to you later on with complaints. It's an important job to keep the communications going and on track. As the salesperson the worst thing you can do is disappear off into the sunset the moment a deal has been done. Relationships are built over time and a long-term collaborative approach is best.

It's also a good idea to fully understand why you have won. Many people forget to do this. What did the client like about you, your company or your pitch? Ask for feedback and share it internally. Make sure you communicate to your team what the key success factors were so that everyone can learn from it. People will often ask for feedback when they have lost a pitch. But most never ask detailed questions about why *they* won. Often, they're just happy and grateful for the work, which is a reasonable position to take – but you could and should go further. Asking why you won will help you replicate your success in other client conversations and achieve a more consistent approach within the business.

Now – go and celebrate, and then make sure you deliver an amazing piece of work for your client!

Summary

Now let's summarise the key elements of the winning client's stage:

The pitch process

Pitching is a broad term that can mean many things, from a one-to-one chat through to a formal process. Don't fear pitches, but welcome them.

Structuring an effective pitch

Understand the fundamentals of the buying funnel. Work out where your target client is and structure your pitch accordingly.

Pricing and valuing your services

Know the market rates and where you fit in. Let your fees reflect the value of you and your business, but ask the client what their budget is.

Negotiation

Know whereabouts on the sliding scale you're negotiating. Understand the bargaining range and where your 'wiggle' room is.

Winning work

Will you use your contract or theirs? What's the agreed time frame? Make sure you are very clear and confident in what your process is so that both of you know the timeline and key project milestones. Don't celebrate too early. Get the contract or purchase order, then celebrate.

Part Three

Growing Your Creative Business

Chapter 9

The final push

Building and maintaining your sales engine

As I mentioned earlier, much of this book was written under global lockdowns, the likes of which were unprecedented and that most of us had never known. They were some of the hardest and challenging moments in my career and working life to date. However, the situation also forced me into taking action, and to adapting new ways of working. It also presented an opportunity for me to write this book – something that had been in the pipeline for a little while beforehand.

In September 2020 I had a trip booked to Amsterdam. I was planning to meet a client on behalf of an agency. Getting on a plane and sitting in the same room as this client felt like the best way to move the conversations forward. Despite all of the uncertainty in the world I booked a ticket to travel, and the client had already agreed to meet.

As I arrived in Amsterdam, Holland was just entering a two-week national lockdown. Covid was running high again and the government had decided to act. So, there I was, on my way to the hotel, completely unsure if this was going to be two days wasted. I had no idea if my client would go ahead with the meeting, nor indeed if I was even going to be allowed to travel home again. The streets of Amsterdam were mostly empty and there was a surreal, but by now familiar, feeling in the city.

I recall checking into Soho House (a great place to stay if you work in the creative sector) and being told that I was one of two people staying there. Two! There are normally 500+. Unable to contact my client I suddenly realised I had an opportunity. I now had an enforced period of time in which to finish writing this book. I was in another country, with no interruptions, nothing in the diary and an inspiring environment (virtually all to myself) in which to write. I spent two days sitting at a desk overlooking the deserted streets of Amsterdam and managed to move this book closer to completion. I had the final push that I needed.

The final push and last stages of any project are often the hardest, and this can be true of sales and new business. Getting clients 'over the line' is often where it can all fall down. Finding ways to mitigate this – such as building a functioning sales engine – are essential to closing and completing your project.

In the end the client did agree to meet me in Amsterdam. The next day I went to his office and had a great one-to-one conversation with him, and we moved things forward. Not only that, but I had also contacted two other clients in Amsterdam prior to travelling and they also agreed to meet. Just a day earlier I'd flown in not knowing if I would see anyone or if it was a wasted trip. Twenty-four hours later, not only had I met three key clients, I'd also nearly completed the first draft of this book.

Often, we never know when opportunities are going to come our way or what they will look like. But when they do, spotting them and taking advantage of them is essential.

Keeping the engine running

Your sales engine is at the very core of your business. It's the driving force that makes everything happen. Without it, your business is going nowhere.

Think of the engine, or more likely these days the electric motor, in your car. It really is the heart of the machine. Without it there will be no forward momentum or movement of any kind. The car is quite literally a pointless lump of metal without an engine, or motor, to propel it. The engine is the most important thing in the vehicle.

If a car has been sitting in a shed or garage for a few years, then the engine or motor will need to be broken down into its major components. Over time each of these will have degraded and started to wear away. In some cases, major parts will be beyond repair and possibly need replacing. Each component must be checked and thoroughly cleaned so that each individual part is sound. Then the engine must be carefully rebuilt and reassembled. It must then be checked and precisely integrated back into the car. Once all of that has happened the engine will need fine-tuning to regain its optimal performance. Only then can the forward motion, energy creation or movement begin. To keep the engine or motor running effectively it must be serviced and tuned on a very regular basis. Then it should run smoothly for long periods of time.

Your sales and new business process is, then, the engine for growth and forward momentum in your business.

Now think about the current sales engine within your business. Is it a highly performing machine? Do you even have one? Is it running at its optimal performance? How often does it get a check-up or service? When was the last time any parts were replaced or upgraded? Is it creating energy and forward momentum for your company?

You might possibly need to take some action if the answer to those questions is not a resounding 'yes'. In previous chapters, we've looked at various elements of the sales process: how to establish a brand proposition, how to strategise and track results, how to audit/ qualify clients, how to generate leads, how to run meetings and have client conversations, how to price your services, and the ways to build high-performing teams . There is a methodology for running highly effective sales campaigns that help quickly grow your business and find new clients. This book has now provided you with a step-by-step guide on how you can rebuild each of the components you need. It also shows you how to assemble them together and how to build a high-performing sales engine within your company. This should be the heartbeat of your business, so keep it serviced and running smoothly.

I have some good news to share with you: it is much easier to keep the momentum going and everything on the right road once the engine is running. Once you've built a sales engine, fired up the motor and have it running then you're more than halfway there. It is far easier to keep things going and improve performance once you've got to this point. Sadly, many agencies never get to this point, which is a large part of why they struggle. They lurch from project to project, either feast or famine commercially. (One week the agency is the busiest place in town, the following week they're sitting around waiting for the phone to ring.) The answer to this is to build a sales engine! This is the thing that is going to propel your business to the next level and beyond.

Here is another little secret: great businesses and business owners instinctively know this. They embed the client conversation at the very heart of what they do. Their sales engines are constantly being looked at. They evaluate them, change them, tweak them, and service them on a regular and consistent basis. These businesses are the ones that thrive while most others just survive. It's what sets apart the good from the great.

So, what do we need to do to keep our sales engine running? How can you break the process down into manageable and simple work areas? What are the key criteria you need to consider and how do you optimise your performance?

There are three key categories that I think need to be viewed and assessed on a regular basis.

These are:

- Team and communication
- Strategy and planning
- Implementation and delivery

Let's look at each in more detail…

Team and communication:
So, congratulations, you've built a sales engine, well done! You have started the process of engaging clients and getting out there to win work. It could just be you in the team as a single sales resource or there could be more than one of you in a team. Whatever your situation it's essential to have a clear understanding of what you're doing, and to regularly review it. Each person in the team must know what is expected of them and be able to clearly communicate that to another person.

Let's look at an example of a small three-to-four-person sales team within a creative business of fifteen to twenty people.

This is a fairly typical set-up in many creative agencies. The first person in the team is likely to be an owner, or founder of the business. This person has probably been assigned the role of owning the entire sales efforts for the business, which could be for a variety of reasons. Usually that they're quite good at it – or (often) nobody else wants to do it! Secondly, there will probably be a Sales or Client Director. This person is usually tasked with leading the charge with new business. There is often a lot of pressure and expectation on them. Finally, there is probably a marketing, lead generator or account manager within the team. Perhaps they are a little more junior but no less important than the other players.

In order to perform as a highly effective, successful sales engine these people need to work extremely well as an integrated unit. Therefore, the communication between them all should be regular, consistent and clear. Each person must understand their own specific objectives and responsibilities. It is no good the founder or owner trying to oversee the marketing or lead generation aspects just because they want to be involved. Their job is to help set the course, design a strategy and create an environment where others can thrive. I know many agency owners that do this well and I also know many who try and involve themselves unnecessarily.

I mentioned that there is a lot of pressure on new business directors. To a point, this is expected. They are often very highly paid, and their job is to bring in revenues. But where it goes wrong is unrealistic targets and a lack of clarity on their expectations. In order for the team to thrive, the new business director must be (relatively!) comfortable with his or her targets. The targets might be challenging but they should not be impossible. There should be some science as to how those targets were set. Were they analytically looked at and forecasted, based on expected revenues, or were they just plucked from thin air? (It happens – and more regularly than you'd think!) Before any targets are signed off everyone should know them, understand them and be confident in them. Only then can there be the kind of relaxed environment that the team needs to succeed. Of course, there should be a healthy amount of pressure and challenge. Not a negative, downbeat set-up whereby everybody (especially the sales director) feels like they're failing week in, week out – that's not an environment where anybody is going to succeed, nor indeed enjoy. This will only serve to create a slightly toxic negative environment. Eventually the founder or owner will get fed up and fire their new business person. Or that person will leave of their own accord. This is a destructive cycle that happens a lot in creative businesses.

As a business owner or team leader, it is highly important that you give people space to do their job. They should feel empowered in their abilities to get the job done. Your team should be enjoying themselves along the way. In turn you should feel confident they can and will deliver alongside you. Isn't that ultimately why you hired them? So – focus on the culture of your organisation. How can you set the framework for these things to happen?

Like many potential problems in life, things can often be solved with communication. Or specifically, *good* communication. When sales teams engage with clarity and regularity things start to shift. People understand on a week-by-week basis what is happening and how they fit in to the overall picture. Having weekly sales 'stand-ups' and meetings will create a forum for communication. (A sales stand-up is a short, ideally punchy, meeting where you connect with your team on a weekly basis to update and share. Note, standing is not mandatory but sometimes encouraged!)

These stand-ups or meetings should be honest, open, warm but direct. It is now easier than ever to do this. Technology means that everyone can join a short call or video conference at least once a week. The purpose of these meetings is very much progress and action updates.

Strategy and planning

On a monthly or quarterly basis take the opportunity to have a broader look at your wider strategy. Are you on track, and is the plan working? Do you need to make any strategic changes?

While the weekly meetings are short, dynamic and action orientated, your monthly or quarterly sessions should be more 'big picture' and strategy focussed. Make sure the entire team is involved in as much of the conversation as possible. Don't exclude some people or shut them out. It's counterproductive and will have a negative effect. Some of the best clients I work with do weekly meetings brilliantly. There is very regular contact: one to ones, strategy sessions and 'off site' meetings. These clients embrace the need to communicate and outline the vision for the company and how it will grow. Crucially, they don't shy away from the difficult subjects that need discussion, such as operational and technical issues, or even client losses. These things are looked at openly and honestly with the entire sales and clients' teams. These agencies have a certain energy, and often, magic about them. I have experienced it on many occasions. I truly believe it starts with their ability to communicate clearly and honestly with their team.

Sales is a team sport. If you can focus on building a high-performing, close-knit business development team it will pay dividends within your company many times over. When each person understands their role and how they contribute, you will be amazed at how quickly your company will grow.

If you are a solo business operator without a team, there are a number of ways you can replicate the effects of a sales team. Involving a third party and sharing your sales plan is a great way to do this, perhaps involving a business mentor or advisor on your quarterly and annual sales campaign. Try to find someone who can become an accountability partner for you. Share your targets and set aside a time to update them on your progress. The more you can involve others in your goals, plans and results, the more accountable you will be to actually go and deliver against the plan. Even a partner or friend is a good person to share it with you if you don't work with any business advisors.

As I mentioned earlier, it is much easier to keep the momentum going once you've begun. Get your team focussed, happy and communicating and the rest will start to take care of itself!

> **Sales Tip 15: Recognise Lady Luck when she visits.**
> Recognise the real opportunities when they come along. Arriving in Amsterdam with two days in lockdown was a strange but welcome chance for me to finish writing these very words. Opportunities will come in all shapes, forms and sizes. Turn on the radar and look out for the ones that are hiding in plain sight. You'll be amazed by the opportunities that you can tune into that will lead to more conversations and fruitful activity for your business.

Implementation and delivery

By now you have planned and strategised. Now it's time to get things done. There is huge satisfaction in doing and delivering. Ultimately of course this is where things actually *happen*. We don't want to be sitting around for weeks on end *thinking* about what we should be doing – we should be out there doing it!

We want to create momentum and give energy to sales activities within the business. Work plans should be organised and focussed so they are highly action-orientated – which means fast delivery, high-impact bursts of activity. It's better to break things down into smaller chunks as opposed to have a daunting list that you don't really make progress with.

What does that mean in practical terms? How are you going to deliver the key elements of your sales campaign? Let's recap on the key elements of an effective campaign from earlier in the book.

These are:

Finding clients

- How do you understand your market and potential client base?
- What do you need to do to qualify them? Why will they work with you?
- Who is the right contact or job profile in their business?

Engaging clients

- What is the most effective way to reach your prospects?
- How do you cut through the noise and ensure your message lands?
- What are their key challenges and how can you align with your services?

Winning clients

- How can you deliver a winning pitch?
- Who will lead the client project and what are the demands on your team?
- What can you learn from the process whether you win, or lose?

These key questions will help shape the way you deliver the various phases of your campaign. I advise you to work through them methodically and sequentially. Often one of the hardest parts is simply getting started and making those first outreaches to clients. But once you've begun, I hope you will see that things flow from there. It's possible to get into a rhythm whereby you are undertaking regular and consistent sales development activities.

These might consist of chunks of time that you allocate to various tasks. It's better to break it down into diary slots of no more than two to three hours at a time. Keep things manageable and achievable. For example, you could try blocking out two hours in the morning to focus purely on client lead generation. This could consist of emails, phone calls or online meetings and essentially any action that is generating activity and new client engagement. Try to avoid answering emails from existing clients or contacts because that is not pure new business – and during those designated two hours you want to stay focussed on new business as much as possible! Carving out regular but dedicated chunks of time is a great way to make progress against your target list. I do it myself on a regular basis to know that I'm constantly generating enough 'reps' or repetitions to build my sales pipeline. I know that if I don't carve out this time then very quickly, I will find myself under pressure.

However you want to look at it, Sales is an action. No action equals no results – and you need results because those results drives business. We have to keep the client development pipeline growing and ticking over. As some clients convert then unfortunately others will fall away. It's just the name of the game and we can't unfortunately win them all. It is often said that 'Sales is a numbers game'. That phrase that is overused and misleading in various ways, and I think it's a crude and rudimentary way to look at the art of Sales. However, there is a degree of truth in it because to ensure a healthy pipeline and stand a chance of some clients converting, you need to generate some *numbers*. But they should have been carefully qualified and evaluated so that you are thinking way beyond it just being 'a numbers game'. It's more sophisticated, more advanced and so must you be in your approach!

> **Sales Tip 16: Target list.**
> Build a target list that is right for your business with the appropriate number of prospects and companies on it. Ten is too few, more than sixty is probably too many realistically. You need to find a level that you can proactively work through. Hence asking yourself "Are these companies really, truly likely to buy from us?" is a very good thing to do.

One of the best bits of advice I ever received in sales was given to me just a few weeks into my first job. I was told by a veteran operations director in an IT company: "Rob, never ever take your foot off the pedal!" You might think this is quite an extreme suggestion and there has to be some balance. However, the principle behind the sentiment is very sound. It was explained to me that it can be very tempting to ease off a little, especially so after a win or success. But when you do that, it becomes twice as hard to regain the position you were in before. For example, you might think: "Great, I've just won a huge project so I can relax for a few months!" But don't do it! You'll find yourself having to work extremely hard to reinvigorate your pipeline and to get back to where you started.

I should add that I have made this mistake several times in my career and always regretted it! So, I'm sharing that advice with you here: *never ever take your foot off the pedal; keep going and keep things consistent.*

The fear factor

Often there is a need to overcome certain obstacles or challenges that you might have in the way. The fear factor. Many people are extremely daunted by the prospect of simply getting started with sales. It's one of the reasons I've written this book. My belief is that we need to reframe the way we look at Sales. Sales as a discipline is not something to be feared or loathed. Rather, it's an exercise that can help you transform your company. However, I recognise that for some people the fear factor is a very real barrier.

In order to overcome any fear, first it must be faced.

It's essential to square up to the 600lb gorilla (fear) who might be trying to dominate and is getting in the way. In fact, squaring up to it is the only way to overcome your fears.

You might want to consider working through some of these questions to help you:

- What am I fearful of when it comes to selling?
- How do I react when I have a positive client conversation?
- How do I react when I have a negative client conversation?
- What feelings does that trigger for me?
- What do I do to avoid sales or new business?
- How regularly do I avoid it and why?
- How do I think clients perceive me and our business?
- What would help me to become more effective and consistent?

Working through these questions is an essential exercise to help you overcome the fear factor. Your answers might surprise you! It could be beneficial to work through the questions with a colleague or friend who can provide an impartial sounding board and perhaps appropriately challenge some of the answers.

This exercise should help you reframe the narrative you have around sales and new business. So that you can focus more on productive client generating activity on a consistent basis. Remember – 80% of success can be put down to showing up. The other 20% is, in various degrees, a combination of hard work, luck, a little talent and creativity!

Celebrate the wins

It's important to celebrate your successes and evaluate your failures. Losing a pitch hurts. A lot! Conversely, winning a pitch or new client is one of the best feelings you can have in any business, especially when you have engineered that opportunity from scratch yourself. So, make the time to learn why you both win and lose projects. Most clients will usually give you open and honest feedback if you take the time to ask for it!

Implementation and delivery is all about momentum and

firing up the sales engine. Wherever possible use the team (or an accountability partner) as much as possible. Create an energy within your business that is explosive and attractive for both clients and colleagues. A reminder that this should be the backbone of your business – the growth engine.

Just remember…'once begun – the job's half done'!

Chapter 10

Troubleshooting

Overcoming challenges

Common problems, client objections, troubleshooting

This section of the book is dedicated to helping you overcome some of the many challenges involved with Sales. It's intended to help you as you get started and begin your sales campaigns. Think of this as the last mile to go in order to really make progress with new clients and conversations.

As we've seen so far, there are many challenges with growing any business or company. If it was easy, then everyone would be doing it and there would be no competition. Unfortunately, though, there is *a lot* of competition out there! There are many agencies and companies who are expert at Sales and new business – and so must you be. However, this is a marathon, not a sprint, so aim to do this over time. It's not realistic to expect instant results. Instead, plan to make steady and incremental gains. Aim for progress, not perfection.

Being aware of some of the common issues and client challenges will help keep things on track. It can be very easy to lose focus or motivation when things don't always go to plan. Which will happen, after all, because it's a fact of life!

The law of averages will dictate that not every conversation or client engagement will always go smoothly. But stay the course and don't give up. Think of clever and innovative solutions and ways around problems. By reading this next section you will have an advantage over most of your competition – this is several decades worth of creative sales experience (and problems!) distilled down and shared for your benefit.

I'm sure you'll face your own problems and objections. No doubt you'll also make a few mistakes along the way – I know I have, but that's okay. In fact, it's probably helpful to do, so that you can understand what works and what doesn't. By looking at some of the common problems, client objections and troubleshooting you'll get a clearer idea of what is happening in your business. Furthermore, you should have some ideas and solutions on how to overcome them.

Internal problems

Some of the biggest problems in Sales can be categorised in five main areas. They are a series of behavioural patterns that can get in the way. However, they are very common to most creative businesses, individuals and salespeople. The good news is there is a workaround for each of them. There are ways you can overcome some of these problems and face them head on. I like to call them the Five Rs:

- Regularity
- Resource
- Relevance
- Recognition
- Reward

Having grouped the Five Rs, let's run through what the problems are and how to face them...

Regularity
- **Not dedicating enough time on a regular basis**
  Carve out the time to dedicate to your sales effort. Twenty minutes a day is better than none!
- **Not following up with clients at the right time**
  Get the balance right. Not every week, don't harass them! Four to six weeks is about right for following up.
- **Setting yourself unrealistic goals**
  Work out small achievable wins, especially as you start. Don't try and climb Everest; first try to conquer the small peaks consistently.
- **Listening to the fear factor**
  Don't let the inner voice take over. We all have it but don't listen to it. Make the time to start and keep it consistent.

Resource

- **A lack of resource**
  Think about what you do have, rather than what you don't.
  Find some time from your week and put your energy into Sales.
- **Using this as an excuse for lack of action**
  Don't fall into the trap of thinking you have no resource or
  time. Only you can make things happen. Find a way!
- **Not knowing how best to use your own time**
  Make a very simple plan and set of goals that you are pursuing.
  Don't complicate it. For example: this month I'll call five new
  clients and talk to them. Simple and focussed.
- **Using your resources in the wrong way, with the wrong
  clients**
  Make sure you use your time and energy in the right way.
  Qualify your prospects. Don't waste time on those who will
  never buy from you. Find the ones who will!

Relevance

- **Not being relevant to your clients**
  You must tailor your messages, content and whole approach.
  It has to be bespoke to them. Spend time crafting emails,
  pitches and key messages.
- **Communications that are not being received**
  Don't send generic content in the hope of success. So-called
  'spray and pray' marketing and sales is dead. Clients are too
  busy to care, and they will ignore you.
- **Failing to cut through and connect**
  Get creative in how you get attention. Be clever, innovative
  and engaging. It takes time to think about, but it works.
  You have to cut through the noise.
- **Forgetting to think like your client**
  Unless you start to think like your client you will struggle
  to be relevant. Put yourself in their shoes. Understand them
  and what they need and frame yourself in the right way.

Recognition

- **Not getting any recognition**

If things are not working, change something. Ask a third party – a colleague, friend or partner. Be objective about what's not working. Experiment and change if needed. Different things work with different clients. Adapt and evolve.

- **Failing to get any successes**
  Reframe what success looks like. Is it a client win, or a client meeting? Give yourself a chance to succeed. Reframe the way you define your successes. They must be achievable.

- **No sales or business wins**
  Why are things not working? What messages are you getting from clients? What can you learn? Repeated losses mean something is wrong – either pricing, people or the whole approach. Understand, get feedback and learn as quickly as you can.

- **Not asking for referrals**
  Most people never ask for referrals. This is a mistake as they are one of the best sources of business. Think about your network, it's more valuable to you than you realise. Think about how you can leverage your clients and wider contact networks.

- **Losing pitches**
  Only go into a pitch believing you can win it. However, if you do keep losing, find out why. Always ask for feedback from the client. Make any changes you need for the next opportunity.

Reward

- **Not rewarding yourself or your team**
  Celebrate your achievements. Remove any negativity and embrace the positive aspects of your efforts. Set yourself a target and reward yourself. Carrot and stick! 'If I do X, then I will allow myself Y'. It's a great way of self-motivating you – or your team.

- **Failing to get balance in the process**
  There must be some balance and perspective here. This is not life and death, nor is it rocket science. We are just trying to grow your company. Keep your expectations right-sized and don't worry too much. Things will work out just fine – if you do the work.

- **Taking time out to step back**
  It's important to step back now and again. Get some disconnection from things. The world is hyper-connected these days, so sometimes disconnecting from business can renew your energy levels and perspective.
- **Not rewarding your client**
  If you win a new client, then firstly you must ensure you deliver on your promises. Make sure the experience of working with you is amazing. Delight – don't disappoint. Have some fun with your clients, too. Take them out, wine and dine when you can and when it's appropriate.

External objections

Clients have their own pressures and demands. This is particularly true in today's turbo-charged, fast-paced global economy. Hyper-connectivity means an 'always on' culture. Despite being told we should have more time, through better communications and connectivity, paradoxically we all seem to have less time. Most people are busy, time poor and often rushed and stressed in many areas of their business lives. Therefore, we have all become skilled at filtering. We filter out what we think we don't need. Some of this happens consciously but much of it happens unconsciously. This filtering process is partly what we're up against when selling. Clients tend to be very good at filtering out. They have a vested interest in protecting the fortunes of their company and are custodians of their business brand.

What does this mean in practical terms for you as the salesperson?

Well, in the same way you've been qualifying your clients, they are doing the same to you. They are constantly looking for reasons *not* to engage with you. In fact, it nearly always starts this way around. Clients will make the case against you first and then (hopefully) slowly reverse that decision over time. Initially, they are looking for signals that they can ignore you. This is the easiest and most effective way that clients filter salespeople. Remember, this filtering process is entirely natural. Don't be put off or made despondent by it. We all do it. Keep in mind it's not personal in any way. It is simply busy clients doing their job. They are trying to qualify you as much as you are them.

Your job is to be consistent and credible. It's essential to build rapport and trust whenever possible. People want to see your staying power. Which in turn demonstrates your seriousness leading to a stable and trustworthy base you can build from. Sometimes it can take six to twelve separate contact points with a client before they'll properly engage with you.

So, with all of this in mind, what are some of the most common client objections and how can you overcome them?

Here are some of the objections I've encountered during my years spent in the creative industry, along with my solutions:

We don't have time to meet

You might have caught the client at the wrong time. If there is no interest or relevance in your approach, then this will often get used as a response. Asking pertinent and relevant questions to understand them better will prevent this from happening.

No budget for this year

Establishing budget should be part of the client qualification process that you go through at the beginning of the conversation. If they are showing interest in you but genuinely don't have budget then fine. Make a note and an agreement to call them back at the right time. However, if there is no budget, period, maybe they aren't the right prospect for you. Your time would be better spent elsewhere.

Not interested

You might find some people are just not interested! There will always be reasons why. Have you qualified and understood them? Are they a relevant client? Is the timing wrong? If they are genuinely not interested, understand why and then move on. You can't win them all!

Send me something and I'll have a look at it

This is a very common client response. It can be interpreted as an objection, and it does put some distance between you and them. Think of ways you can avoid sending something. Suggesting a meeting instead. Or a second call to present some ideas. Sending something isn't always an objection or a 'no'. However, try to avoid it where possible. You want to keep the conversation and engagement going in other ways.

You're too expensive

Another very common objection. It's important to fully understand your client or prospect. Do they have the capacity and budget to buy your services? You must know this before engaging with them. Often the answer will be 'no'. Remember, it's not always a problem being expensive. In fact, it can be a good thing. If you're 'best in class' then help them realise that. Don't be afraid to sell at a premium. The best brands in the world do it. Have confidence in your prices and your client's ability to pay for it.

You're too cheap

An interesting one! A client might not say this to your face, but many will think it. If you are dramatically undercutting the market and competition, it will raise serious questions. Clients could doubt your credibility and your viability. They may even wonder if you will stay in business long enough to deliver their project. Pricing your services correctly is essential.

We don't like the idea

This is one of the most disheartening things a client will say to you, especially after a pitch. Sometimes they like *you* but not your *idea*. In this situation, you need to refocus and reconnect with them to understand why. Ask questions to get to the bottom of what they really want and quickly. (Ideally this should have happened at the outset.)

Our team likes it, but we need to present to senior management

It's vital that you understand the various stakeholders involved from the get-go. You don't want to get stuck at a certain level of the business or behind certain gatekeepers. You need to involve all key decision makers from the outset. How do you do that? Ask! Be clear and confident in asking at an early stage: "What needs to happen for this to proceed, and who needs to be involved?"

We have a roster of companies

And you're not on it! Some companies have a watertight roster and there is no deviation from that. In which case it might be best to move on. However, there is often scope to work outside of the roster. Many individuals don't like to be restricted to just a few companies. They will champion other suppliers. Find those clients!

I've never heard of your company

This is all about building trust and credibility. How you position yourselves as expert and knowledgeable in your field. To counter this, you need to demonstrate your experience and ability. Perhaps you're the challenger brand to market leaders? Clients want to hear a clear and concise story about you and your business. Make it fun, relevant and engaging.

Your product or service can't do X,Y,Z

Clients will often present barriers, challenges and obstacles in relation to your product or service. Identify them as quickly as possible. Work through them in a collaborative way with the client. Ideally, they should be helping you to work around any problems and find solutions, because it's to their benefit as well as yours.

We're working with another vendor – we're very happy with them

Always remain inquisitive and interested. Why do they like their incumbent supplier and what's working well? Look for gaps or opportunities and bide your time. Perhaps it's best to agree to speak again in six months' time. Enter it into your CRM so you have a reminder to circle back round.

I don't see how your service could help us

Recognise here that you've not aligned yourself with their needs or wants. You might have failed to qualify the client or business entirely. Are they a genuine prospect for you?

Your product is too complicated

You don't ever want to hear this! It means you have either confused them, or worse, bored them so they've tuned out. Make your proposition so ridiculously simple that anybody could understand it.

Avoid jargon. Put yourself in the client's shoes before you talk to them or pitch to them. Start with the basics and the USPs, and build from there.

I'm busy

If you're hearing this, you've got the timing completely wrong. Always listen out for the signals a client is giving you. If they're busy, or sound like it, suggest another time to speak. You want them in a relaxed and open frame of mind.

You're annoying me, go away

It's gone wrong! You should never annoy or bore. Ever.

F*@k off!

It's gone very, *very* wrong. Ideally, never ever get to this point! But it might not be you – it could be them. If they're this rude, and you haven't done anything to warrant it, then maybe they're not the right target for you and are best avoided.

Further Troubleshooting

The best laid plans do not always work. There are times when things just don't seem to go your way. Here are some additional solutions to common problems that you might encounter.

I can't get through to the right client

It can be extremely frustrating when you are trying to reach a specific contact or person. You know they're the right profile, but you just can't reach them. Often the key here is to change something. Do things differently. So, if you've been calling them, try an email or vice versa. Send them something unexpected that's likely to get their attention. A very well written, old-fashioned letter can often work. Or ask for a referral from someone else in the business. Step back and consider what it is that will make this person respond. Ask yourself: "How can I engage them and make it so relevant to them that they won't ignore the approach?" Get creative and innovative!

I'm struggling with the gatekeepers

Gatekeepers could be anyone from receptionists through to PAs and project managers. Essentially, a gatekeeper is anyone who is in between you and the decision maker. The mistake most salespeople make is to treat these people as if they were the enemy. They are not. They are your friend. My suggestion is to see them as someone who can help you connect with the right client. If you are highly credible and take the time to explain *why* you want to speak to the person, invariably the gatekeeper will help you. Most people like to help if you ask nicely and are professional.

Clients keep saying 'no' to meetings

As mentioned earlier, clients are expert at filtering out and qualifying. Their standard default is often to say 'no' to any meeting requests, in which case avoid the temptation to be persistent and pushy. Instead, ensure your initial conversation or approach is highly relevant and unique so that you avoid getting a 'no' to your meeting requests. Change the approach or change your pitch so that it's so punchy and compelling that clients are prepared to meet or have a further conversation. You can also suggest times or days when you will be near their office. This is also a helpful 'nudge' to make it easier for the client. Make it ridiculously easy for them to say 'yes'. Suggest thirty minutes instead of an hour, for example.

We keep losing pitches

If you are in this situation, then clearly things are not working in the right way. Something is fundamentally flawed with your whole Sales approach. After a lost pitch, always ask for feedback on why you lost. Keep notes so that if it happens a lot you can analyse: are there any common themes? For example, does budget come up in more than one of these lost pitches? Look carefully at the feedback because it usually comes down to a few key categories as to why companies win or lose. Before you undertake any pitch or proposal, you must qualify that client. Are they right for you and your business? Will they engage and talk to you? Do they have the right budgets? A failure to qualify at the start will lead to repeated lost pitches. It's frustrating, costly and soul-destroying for all involved. So, break out of the habit and reclaim the balance of power back in *your* favour. You do this by asking questions, qualifying and, occasionally, saying 'no'. There's no harm in qualifying *yourself* out, and deciding not to go for a particular pitch in the first place because you know you're not likely to win it.

We're not winning any work

There are many reasons why you might not be winning work. Understanding the key factors – fast – is essential. Ask your clients and peers for feedback. Try to frame the success factors of your Sales efforts in the right way. Ultimately, it's about winning work and generating revenues. However, what are the milestones along the way? It might be engaging three to five new clients in initial conversations, *before* you sell them anything. Think about the smaller successes and give yourself some easier wins to start with. It's much easier to climb the stairs step by step than it is to climb a mountain. Keep things right-sized and achievable. Winning work will flow from there eventually. Unfortunately, there are no short cuts! Only a methodical and structured approach as outlined in Part Two of the book.

I'm just not motivated to start selling

Being in the right space is essential to your success. With the right attitude and motivation, you can achieve anything, but without it you won't make any progress. Think about what's holding you back. Have you set realistic goals? What can you change? Keep them small and manageable. Think about the times of the day or week when you are more motivated or effective. Repeat those and diarise so there is regularity. Involve a third party, either a colleague, friend or partner. Share the pressure and don't keep it all internalised with you. You're also creating some accountability so that the person will hold you to, and help encourage you, with those small regular goals. Remember 'progress not perfection' here. Making a start is the first big step. Reward your successes and analyse your failures.

I don't know where to start

Hopefully, reading this book has been a good start for you, and you now know where to start. But if you still don't feel confident – begin at the end! Or rather, begin with your end goal in mind. What are you trying to achieve? Where do you want to get to? Map out the sales journey from A to B to C. Is that realistic for your business? Once you've identified your goal, you can begin to build a sales strategy and plan to implement it. Sometimes you just have to take a deep breath and start!

Our team are not selling anything

If you have a poorly performing Sales team, then clearly something is fundamentally wrong. Diagnose what it is. Is it the personalities involved? Is it their sales pitch and key messages? Perhaps the problem is the leadership of that team? It's rare to have an entire team who are not selling anything. Examine yourself too because it might be you who needs to make some changes. Do you need to be clearer about the expectations or set more realistic targets?

We only win small clients

This is a very common problem for small creative agencies. How do you secure the game-changer clients – the ones with bigger budgets which will help you grow? There are two factors which can help. The first is to grow with your clients. Starting small is not always a problem if those businesses have the potential to grow. They *may* carry you along with them on their journey. The second idea is to work up to the bigger clients. Obviously, don't try and pitch straight to Google or Apple – pick some mid-sized (but still substantial) businesses along the way. These 'challenger brands' are a great way of working up to larger clients over time. Your chances of success will be far greater. Eventually you will be in a position to go for larger and larger projects and go for the major clients. Build up to it.

I don't know which clients to target

Do your homework here. Start with the low-hanging fruit first. You ideally want the clients who are going to give you the quickest possible returns for your business. Think about the profile of who that might be. Start there and build your pipeline with these companies. Perhaps existing relationships or even lapsed clients are best? They are much easier conversations than those with new logos. Think about the quickest results and impact for your business first and foremost.

I can't find any information on my prospects

There is a wealth of information out there these days. From LinkedIn and other social media, to general business information from company websites. It's essential to research the client and prospect thoroughly. Take the time to understand the landscape of an organisation. What are their key challenges? Are there press articles or company updates that help give you information? Knowledge is power so take the time to get that information. Get creative with it! Do some digging and proper research. It will pay dividends.

My emails get ignored

Most clients are deluged with emails. Email marketing or lead generation is unfortunately a fairly blunt tool in your arsenal. However, it can be effective when deployed in the right way. Most people send incredibly bland and boring emails which simply get ignored and deleted. You have to write the email whilst constantly thinking like the client you are sending it to. Why should they care? What will get their attention? If your emails are being ignored, they are, sadly, too boring and not relevant. Change the style to write in their language. Use 'you' rather than 'we' wherever possible. Make it about them – not about you!

They don't respond well in meetings

If you find clients are not responding well in meetings, then you are possibly confusing them. You should lead with a clear and simple sales message. That should be well rehearsed and flow off the tongue so that it's easy to understand. Client time is difficult to secure. Any meeting you have is a golden opportunity to build the relationship, so don't waste it. Do your preparation. Set a clear agenda and frame the outcomes upfront. Deliver a clear and concise message that is *relevant* to them.

We don't have any leads to focus on

If you are starting from scratch then it's likely you'll have few leads or ongoing client conversations. However, don't be disheartened by this. We all have to start somewhere! Even experienced sales professionals were in the same situation at some stage in their career. The goal is to build your new business pipeline, carefully and methodically. The pipeline will come together over a few months once you take the time to reach out to your target list with a credible and relevant approach. Remember to keep the goals achievable and manageable. Eventually your lead generation will yield results and you can build the pipeline step by step. Don't be put off starting from scratch. We've all done it!

I can't keep up with progress or sales info

Once you're up and running you must keep track of your leads and conversations. It's essential to capture everything in a CRM system. That could be as sophisticated as the latest Salesforce software or as basic as a spreadsheet. Don't squander all that hard work and effort by failing to follow up. If a client asks for a call back in two months' time – make sure you do it! So many people forget or lose track of these conversations. You must track (and review) your progress to ensure you're delivering against your strategy.

Work and project delivery gets in the way

Many agencies and creatives allow 'the work' to take over, especially when things get busy. It's an easy mistake to make and very common. However, you must, must, must find a way to avoid falling into this trap. Once you do it's very hard to get out of again, and it will hold you back from consistent growth and progress. Try to delegate delivery as much as possible to project teams. Only you can ensure that the Sales and new business efforts are embedded at the core of your company. Remember: it's the main thing that separates the good from the great! So, don't get bogged down in the weeds – stay focussed on new business, sales and winning clients!

There are many reasons as to why you might not be getting the results you want. I have tried to share as many of the common problems here. Some of them might be totally unique to your business. Wherever possible try to avoid them becoming insurmountable obstacles. Cut yourself free from the shackles and find a way around the problem. There is nearly always a solution when you look at things objectively and creatively.

Finally, a word on time. Time is the single biggest asset in your business. In your life, in fact. It would be a mistake to think you don't have enough of it. Or that you are too busy on other things to make time for new business. You must find the time. Carve out small chunks wherever you can. Regularly and consistently. Look at the things that hold you back. What is stopping you and why?

Sales Tip 17: Big rocks!
Carve out the time for the big stuff, not the small stuff. Time management is essential. I recommend looking at *The 7 Habits of Highly Effective People* by Stephen R Covey. There are many great videos on YouTube covering the 'Big Rocks Time Management' idea. Including one brilliantly 90s version with Covey himself. Get the big rocks done and the smaller details will always take care of themselves. Have a watch – it's transformational!

When you make the time in your business the money will follow. Time, when used correctly, can be a cash generator.

To quote the great film composer Hans Zimmer: "The seconds of your life are ticking away". This is a man whose art and craft is all about keeping time. He's an expert in time. So must you be. You only have a finite amount of time to make a difference, to implement change, to start and take action. Everyone has the same amount of time each week. It's purely down to you how you use it. Time is the most precious resource there is.

So, now's the time – let's get going!

Final tips for (sales) performance

In order to implement some of the ideas in the preceding chapters there are a few obstacles that you must be aware of. These are not necessarily client problems or even business problems. Rather, they are more likely to be personal things to you in your life. We must understand some of the common pitfalls and barriers that will often come up. These things could prevent you from maximising your sales efforts and getting the most out of your time. We want to avoid that from happing as much as possible. To grow your business, you need to give yourself the best chance of success and to remain in a consistently high-performing state.

In many ways consistency is the key. That is what you are striving for. When you're inconsistent it hampers your progress and slows things down. It can be one step forward and then two steps back – and I speak from experience here. There have been many times in my career where I have not always been consistent. When I reflect back, I can see that at times not having a consistent or steady approach has been a blockage in terms or performance and pure results.

There are a number of reasons why this happens. Certainly, there were a number of reasons for me. The swings in inconsistency can be huge. Some days it can feel like you're a business genius, overcoming any problem and winning clients left, right and centre. The next week you're sitting there feeling confused, demotivated and overwhelmed. I've been there. It's human nature to have peaks and troughs of performance. Our behaviours will, of course, change over time. This can even happen from day to day. This is completely normal, predictable and understandable because we're human beings. However, an inconsistent approach with work and performance is something slightly different. If we allow certain things (more of which below) to get in the way then we will generate inconsistent results.

Like I said, one step forward, two steps back. It's like climbing the mountain and then base jumping off it only to find that you must climb the mountain all over again. We want to stay up at the peak, or somewhere near there, for as long as possible. Why make it any harder for yourself?

It's also important to stay focussed on the task in hand. To not get distracted by either successes, or failures. New business takes time. It takes time to work through the process and methods I've outlined and to build an effective sales campaign that is unique to your business. Don't be disheartened if it takes a little longer than you expected. Keep going and don't be tempted to break out or diverge into other areas. Knowing and setting your shared sales goals will help you to do this. You can plot a course and a time frame that you think it will realistically take you to get there. The important thing is to keep going!

Let's look at some of the key things that can hold you back. The things that often get in the way. Not just with sales but in lots of other areas in life!

Motivation

Naturally this is something that will fluctuate. With the best will in the world nobody can be 100% fully motivated all of the time. If you are then I congratulate you. I find I can't work like that but, thankfully, I am fully motivated for the *majority* of the time. Even when writing a book! But I do have days where my energy levels and motivation are less than ideal and I'm okay with that. It's just human nature. Recognise and understand when that happens for you. To acknowledge it and give yourself permission to have an off day. However, it's taken me a number of years to recognise this and to give myself permission to be okay with it. Most people tend to be quite hard on themselves and I was often that way myself, saying things like: "I should be doing more", or "I'm not getting the results". When these days come try acknowledging it. Instead of working on your Sales campaign, perhaps do something easier. Some admin or any other general business tasks you might need to do. The key is to not get bogged down in the negativity. Don't get sucked into the vortex of failure just because of a dip in motivation. It will happen, and you can get through it. Personally, when I allow myself the time and space, then the opposite happens. I come back feeling renewed and revitalised, having recognised I needed to do something different for a little while. It works – if you let it!

Peers

What does your peer support network look like? Who are your closest business colleagues? Do you have mentors or people you look up to and learn from? Who do you turn to for advice, especially when things get challenging? Are your family and friends supportive of what you're doing? Hopefully you have positive answers to these questions. It's vitally important to surround yourself with the right people for you and your business. People who know and understand you. Who can appropriately challenge you and ask direct questions when needed. We all need people who can help hold us to account and keep things on track. Nothing great in business was ever achieved in isolation. Sales is a team sport so assemble the best possible network you can. Spend as much time as possible among other successful entrepreneurs and businesspeople. Most will help you if you ask. You will learn and grow from these people hugely.

The phone

A scourge of our modern world. We have lost control of our time and attention to the phone. You only have to look around to realise this. People these days are glued to their phones. Any form of screen in fact. I feel that screen time and digital addiction is probably the next big public health issue, in the same way smoking and drinking were decades ago. The phone, or rather minicomputer, is a wonderful and powerful tool. However, fundamentally, it is a huge distraction. It will take your time and attention away from truly constructive and effective tasks. Social media doesn't help either. There is always something to check, scroll, read or post. My biggest suggestion here is take back the power from your phone. Make it work for you and not the other way around. Try turning the notifications off so they don't appear on the home screen. You'll be amazed at the difference this makes. When working on a few hours of dedicated Sales time, try leaving the phone in another room or a drawer and use a landline if possible. The constant breaks in your attention will interrupt your flow and hinder your progress.

Distractions

We now live in a hyper-connected world. A culture of 'always on' has taken over. Most people have their work email on their phone and it constantly pings away during the day. Even after hours. This is not a healthy situation. It creates numerous distractions throughout the day that will take you away from the task in hand. Such as finding and engaging clients in the appropriate way! The goal is to try and minimise these day-to-day distractions as much as possible. Try to avoid working at the top of your inbox answering emails as they come in. In fact, I often close my emails entirely when working on important tasks (such as writing these very words) and when working towards my daily goals. Instead, step back and work on those big game-changing goals that you have set yourself. There will always be time to send emails, reply to texts or look at social media. You can do that later or at set times during the day. Think about the specific things in your life that distract you. How can you mitigate and avoid them? Dial down the distractions, because the more you can focus, the better your results will be.

Environment

Look around at your workspace. What environment and work setting are you in? Perhaps you're working from a coffee shop or your kitchen table? There is nothing wrong with that per se. We all have to start somewhere. I've done lots of work in coffee shops and still do occasionally. However, your location will define your results. A co-working space is a much more conducive environment for success. You will be surrounded by other like-minded companies, start-ups and entrepreneurs. This will help energise you to continue and focus. Think about the people who are in your working location. Hosting your client meetings in a members' club or a high-end hotel is better than meeting at a local café. Your workspace can genuinely determine your results, so find the right location and watch your results dramatically improve. To quote Daniel Priestley: "Environment Dictates Performance".

Your headspace

How often do we find ourselves in the right headspace? Does that niggling negative voice sometimes get in the way? It's critical to find some balance with your mindset and approach to new business. New business isn't always an easy task and sometimes the mind throws little obstacles in our way. It says things like: "I can't be bothered to do that" or "I'll do something else today". Try to recognise the negative voice and the associated behaviour patterns when they come. The acclaimed sports psychologist Dr Steve Peters calls it the 'chimp theory', whereby the primitive part of your brain (the 'chimp') tries to run riot and ruin things at critical times. Perhaps you can relate to some of that behaviour? If so, spend some time considering when your headspace is at its best. For some, that's first thing in the morning, while for others it's mid-afternoon. Identify your best time of day and use it.

Meditation

Meditation is a great help with staying in the right headspace. It was a game-changer for me. I now use a simple app to do a ten- or fifteen-minute meditation each morning. My day is hugely more effective as a result. It's now as important as taking a shower and having my breakfast each day. It makes that *big a difference* in my ability to focus, concentrate on one thing at a time and (generally) stay in the right headspace. Meditation can help unlock the creative thinking process and allow you to use the mind better. It's also been proven to improve the hippocampus part of the brain which is associated with memory and recall – which means you'll remember more of your clients' faces, names and more about them overall. I can vouch for the fact that this is true! Working with creativity and sales is intense – and meditation can help you stay present, grounded and focussed.

Self-care

We all need to practise a little self-care on a regular basis. We're supposed to be more connected and working less due to new technologies. Yet most people are plugged into the mainframe all day, every day. Paradoxically, people are working harder than ever before. They're wired in and always on with a constant stream of video calls, meetings and client work. It's exhausting! The need for self-care is more important than ever. Give yourself some time out on a regular basis. Some space to unwind and… disconnect! Which means no emails, no calls and ideally no phone! A healthy diet, good sleep and exercise are all key to a good self-care routine. Business efficiency could be vastly improved if the world did this a little bit more.

Alcohol or drugs

Make sure you have a good relationship with these things. Do you find they sometimes get in the way? If so, they might be a problem you need to look at. The creative industry is an exciting and often intoxicating world. There is always a party to go to or someone to have a drink with. But if you are out every night at the heart of the party, can you get up the next day and perform in your business? It's not essential to have drinks with your clients and there are other ways of building deep and lasting relationships without having to go and get drunk with them. A game of tennis or golf is a great alternative. Or invite them to breakfast, dinner or an event. Make sure partying, booze or drugs are not holding you back. If you can remove these obstacles your business will fly.

Being too nice or too polite!
If we are going to get client projects over the line you will need an ability to close. That final 5%–10% push that closes the deal. I always advocate a polite and professional approach. (Never anything less, in fact.) However, on occasion, you will need to find that killer instinct to close projects down and win the work. It can feel uncomfortable and unnatural, but you have to do it because if you don't then somebody else will; probably one of your competitors. Don't be afraid to ask for the business. Remember that great simple question: "What do we have to do to win the work?" I've never had a bad reaction to this question, and I ask it a lot. There will come a point where the client will expect you to do it and you *need* to do it. Don't be *too* nice. Close the work – nothing will happen until you do.

Financial management

You've done it! You've won the work. It's a game-changing project and brings in significant revenue for your company. How will you manage the numbers? Are you confident financially? Does the budget scare you? Good financial management is essential in your sales efforts. You're expected to know the numbers you are pitching to your client and be able to answer competently and effectively. If those numbers have a direct impact on your turnover or profitability, then make sure you understand the financial implications of each project or deal. If you're not a numbers person, employ someone who is. There are now a host of accountants and accountancy platforms out there who can help you do this more easily. If the numbers scare you, get some help!

A word on trust
I have saved the final section of this book for a word on trust. It is the single most valuable commodity you have as a salesperson. When you gain the trust of another person the path to growth and new business will effortlessly open up in front of you. Without trust you have nothing, and you face an impossible task.

As we saw earlier in the book, Sales has built up a bad reputation over the years. Many industries have contributed to this slow build-up of negativity. The problem has pervaded popular opinion that Sales automatically equals lack of trust. I don't believe this is fair or true. These are one of the many reasons why I decided to write this book. The art of selling does not deserve its negative reputation. Many of the world's biggest businesses are trusted to sell to you every day. We don't give it a second thought and we allow them to do it. Why, then, on an individual level are we wary of salespeople? The real expert salespeople in creative companies are game-changers. Rainmakers who can deliver major growth for their businesses. They are celebrated and trusted by their colleagues and employers. This is what we must become. Expert and trusted by colleagues and clients.

I believe that trust underpins everything we do, not just in business but also in life. It is the ultimate currency. But like any currency it must be earned. It is rarely gifted, certainly not in any large quantities. It has to be earned and built over time.

If you follow the suggestions and methodologies in this book, you will build your own trust creation process. It is designed to help you listen, identify, engage and respond – and then to help you take action to deliver your true value to your clients. You can think of Sales as simply a 'trust creation process', one that you methodically work through on a consistent and repeated basis.

Your success will come down to your ability to build trust. To show people that you are not to be feared but instead to be listened to. That you have genuine value to offer them. That you are interested in them. That you want to know what is going on in their world. That you genuinely care. That you can connect and *build connections* with people. To not be in it purely for your own gains, material or otherwise.

Trust is your biggest asset. Build your trust and the rest will follow.

Summary and close

Thank you for reading this book. I hope you've enjoyed it and are ready to implement many of the ideas and suggestions I've put forward. They are built on years of experience, many successes – and also a lot of failures along the way! I hope by now I have built your trust as a Sales expert who can help your business with some of these strategies.

You may need to revisit this book from time to time. It's been designed in a way that you can dip in and out of it as you need. The process and methodologies are to help you build a high-performing sales engine within your business. The framework I've set out is proven to help grow creative companies and can be implemented by you for your clients. It will help you cut through the noise and grow – quickly!

Sales is not something to be feared. New business should be celebrated as the game-changer that it truly is for many creative companies. When it's embraced and done well agencies and creatives thrive. I hope this book is the first step on that journey to growth. Slowly, over time, we can start to reframe the way we see Sales. And perhaps our attitudes can shift to a more positive view and outlook on Sales generally.

So good luck, and I wish you the best in your endeavours as you grow your business.

Sales needs a Rebrand!

Rob

Rob King
The Client Key – *www.theclientkey.com*
Find me on social:
Instagram: @rob.king.agencies and @theclientkey
LinkedIn: Rob King – The Client Key

Acknowledgements

There are numerous people to thank for their support with this book.

Firstly to some of my brilliant clients in no particular order: Pete Stevenson and Phil Blundell at The Edge Picture Company; two giants of their industry and master salesmen who have both taught me so much and been the source of inspiration for more than a decade. The board and my friends at The Edge for creating such a wonderful place and successful agency to be a part of. Steve Songaila for his counsel, friendship and support. Martin Finn and Nick Fuller at EdComs, two more giants of their particular industry. The legendary Kev Chesters, Paul Hammersley, Mick Mahoney and everyone at Harbour. Ritam Gandhi and David Grenham at Studio Graphene. Sinead, Jamie and Alistair at LogicLogicMagic.

The wonderful Hazel May, the advertising industry's best-kept secret. A big thank you to Gary Fitzpatrick, Peter Litten and Angela Law for taking a chance on me and ultimately starting the process of Selling Creativity. Andrew Harvey and Steve Quah at Cheerful Twentyfirst for keeping the show going.

Dave Holley at Abbey Road Studios for making the music dream come true and another music chapter to be continued. Thanks also to Tim Clarke and Lucy Pullin at ie:music and ie:entertainment.

Some personal thank yous particularly with this book: Amy Bedford for her help, research and overall brilliance as a colleague, and Jordan Golebiowski for his talent, ability to get stuff done and make things happen at the ripe old age of just 21.

A special mention to Liz Ward who was the accountability and continual nudge I needed to get this book finished. You were there right from the outset and ultimately kept me going to the finish line. Thank you, Liz.

Daniel Priestley for inspiring so many businesses and entrepreneurs to build, grow and think big. Helen Hart at SilverWood Books who helped take this book from draft to completion with her expertise and input across the many steps along the way. To Lyn McLeod and Tess Mion for being the first people to read the original draft and both giving me the reassurance I needed.

To Nicky Walton Flynn for helping cut off the shackles. Without her help, this book would never have happened and I would not be living the life I am today.

Finally to Vanessa, for putting up with me constantly telling her to go away whilst writing this book in lockdown. For the love, support, fun and general joy in my life with our beautiful family.

Thank you, all.

Milton Keynes UK
Ingram Content Group UK Ltd.
UKHW010138120424
440788UK00001B/5